Short & Easy Manuals Collection

**kevin
mayhew**

kevin mayhew

First published in Great Britain in 2002 by Kevin Mayhew Ltd
Buxhall, Stowmarket, Suffolk IP14 3BW
Tel: +44 (0) 1449 737978 Fax: +44 (0) 1449 737834
E-mail: info@kevinmayhewltd.com

www.kevinmayhew.com

© Copyright 2002 Kevin Mayhew Ltd.

The music in this book is protected by copyright and may not be reproduced
in any way for sale or private use without the consent of the copyright owner.

9 8 7 6 5 4 3 2 1

ISBN 978 1 84003 878 1
ISMN M 57024 007 4
Catalogue No. 1400321

Cover design: Sara-Jane Came

Printed and bound in Great Britain

Contents

Adagio	Christopher Tambling	44
A little jaunt	Andrew Moore	124
Andante	Johann Rinck	103
Andante from Sonatina	Jacob Schmitt	40
Andante tranquillo	Gregory Murray	82
Andante tranquillo	Andrew Moore	118
Andantino	César Franck	72
A prayer of peace	Michael Higgins	98
A prayer song	Andrew Moore	58
Aria	Noel Rawsthorne	56
Aria	Richard Lloyd	76
Arietta	John Marsh	80
Arioso	Noel Rawsthorne	100
A sad piece	Andrew Moore	24
A short recessional	Andrew Moore	16
A tuba minuet	Christopher Tambling	90
Calm reflection	Colin Mawby	20
Cantabile	Simon Clark	108
Canzona	Gregory Murray	114
Chant de matin	Léon Boëllmann	70
Communion prelude	Michael Higgins	30
Country minuet	Graham Knott	104
Cradle song	Richard Lloyd	86
Diludium	Richard Lloyd	116
Domine clamavi	Philip Moore	50
Elegy	Michael Higgins	122
Evening calm	Eduard Schütt	128
Festal day	Elizabeth Hill	48
Hail the dawn	Colin Mawby	38
Idyll	Edward MacDowell	96
Improvisation	Andrew Moore	67
Interlude	Adolf Hesse	8
Interlude	Noel Rawsthorne	105

Interlude	Léon Boëllmann	120
Invocation	Alexandre Guilmant	32
La Furstemberg	Michel Corrette	88
Laudate!	Colin Mawby	110
Mallaby-Deeley's march	Richard Lloyd	60
Meditation	James Patten	28
Meditation at Engelberg	John Marsh	64
Minuet	Georg Böhm	12
Minuet	Joseph Haydn	17
Morning light	Andrew Moore	6
Nobilmente	Andrew Moore	74
Our Lady's morning song	Stanley Vann	52
Pastorale	Elizabeth Hill	36
Pastorale	Léon Boëllmann	84
Prayer	Alexandre Guilmant	112
Prayer to the Trinity	Andrew Moore	79
Prelude	Louis Lefébure-Wély	5
Prelude	Gustav Merkel	66
Prelude	Zdeněk Fibich	102
Prelude in B♭	Johann Rinck	46
Prelude in C	César Franck	42
Prelude in C	Carl Nielsen	85
Prelude in D minor	Anton Bruckner	94
Prelude in E minor	Alexandre Boëly	34
Prière	César Franck	78
Procession to a jaunty tune	Rosalie Bonighton	62
Promenade	June Nixon	92
Reflection	Betty Roe	126
Rejoice greatly	John Marsh	26
Siciliano	Elizabeth Hill	14
Slow air	Samuel Wesley	54
Stately sortie	Andrew Fletcher	10
Strophe	Alexandre Guilmant	95
The Vines	Norman Warren	18
To a wild rose	Edward MacDowell	22
Trumpet tune	David Terry	106
Voluntary	William Croft	68

PRELUDE

Louis Lefébure-Wély (1817-1869)

MORNING LIGHT

Andrew Moore

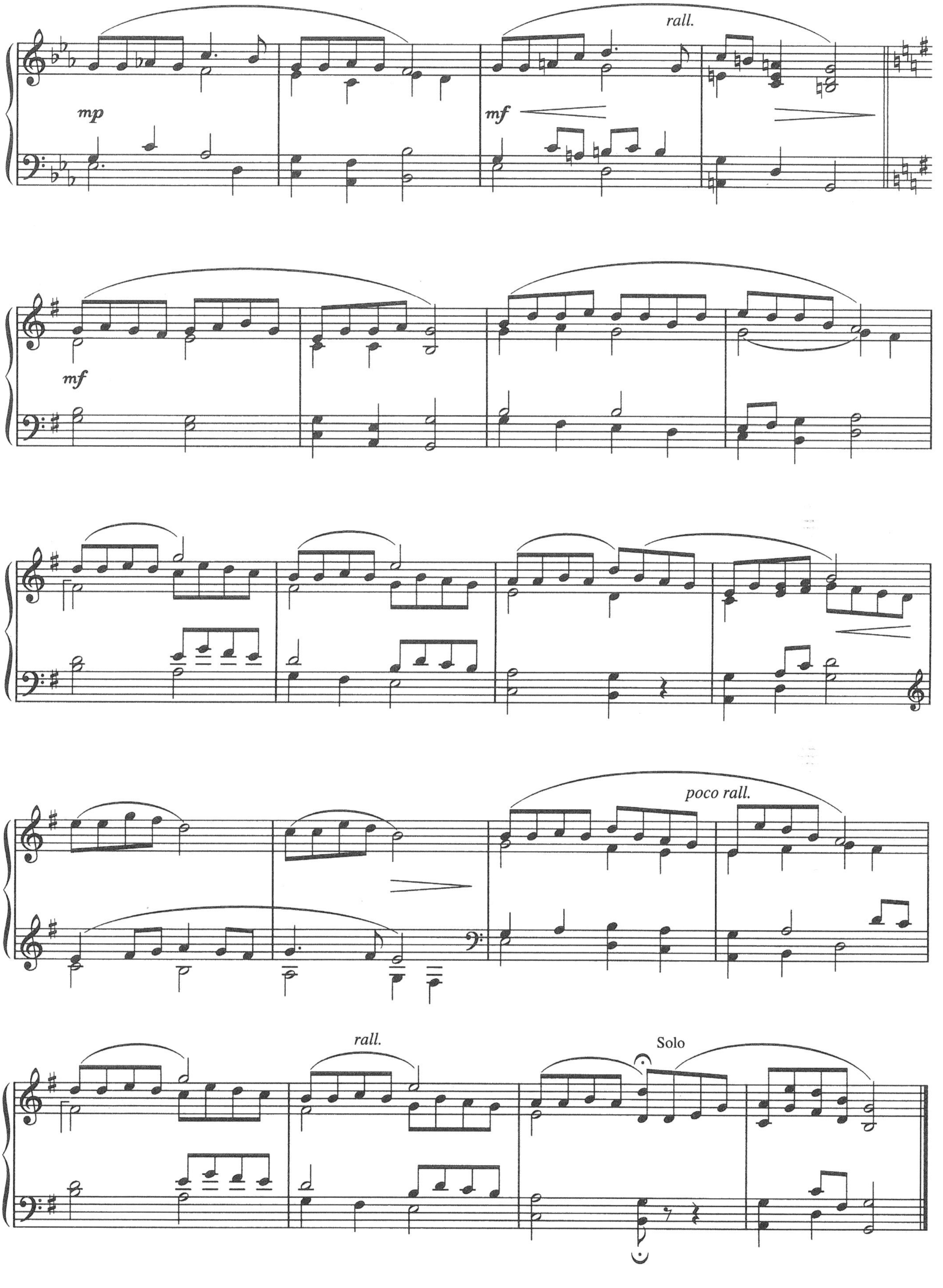
rall.
mp
mf
mf
poco rall.
rall.
Solo

INTERLUDE

Adolf Hesse (1809-1863)
arr. Alan Ridout

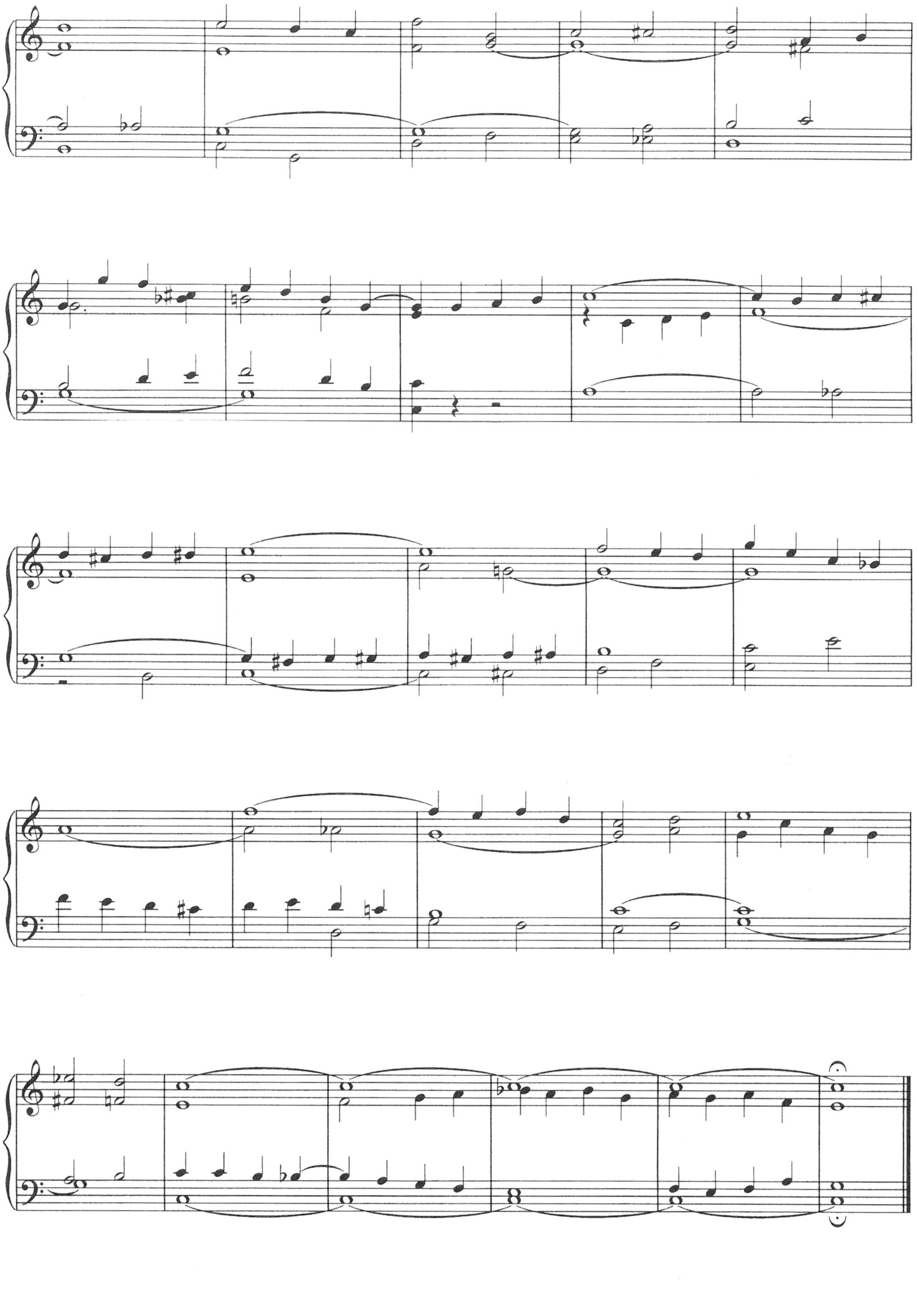

STATELY SORTIE

Andrew Fletcher

poco rall.

MINUET

Georg Böhm (1661-1733)

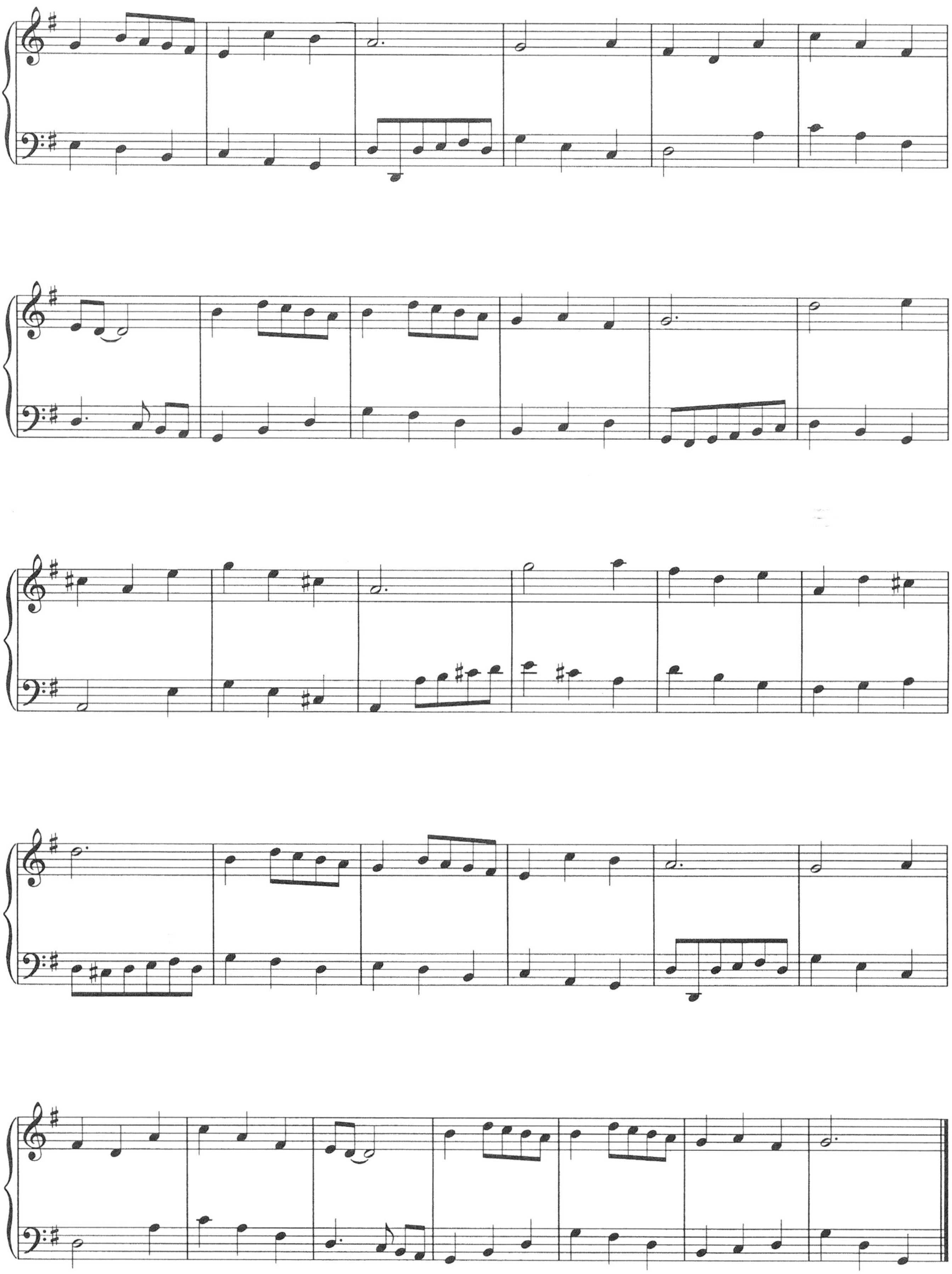

SICILIANO

Elizabeth Hill

15

A SHORT RECESSIONAL

Andrew Moore

MINUET

Joseph Haydn (1732-1809)

THE VINES

Norman Warren

19

CALM REFLECTION

Colin Mawby

© Copyright 1993 Kevin Mayhew Ltd.
It is illegal photocopy music.

21

TO A WILD ROSE

Edward MacDowell (1860-1908)

© Copyright 1993 Kevin Mayhew Ltd.
It is illegal photocopy music.

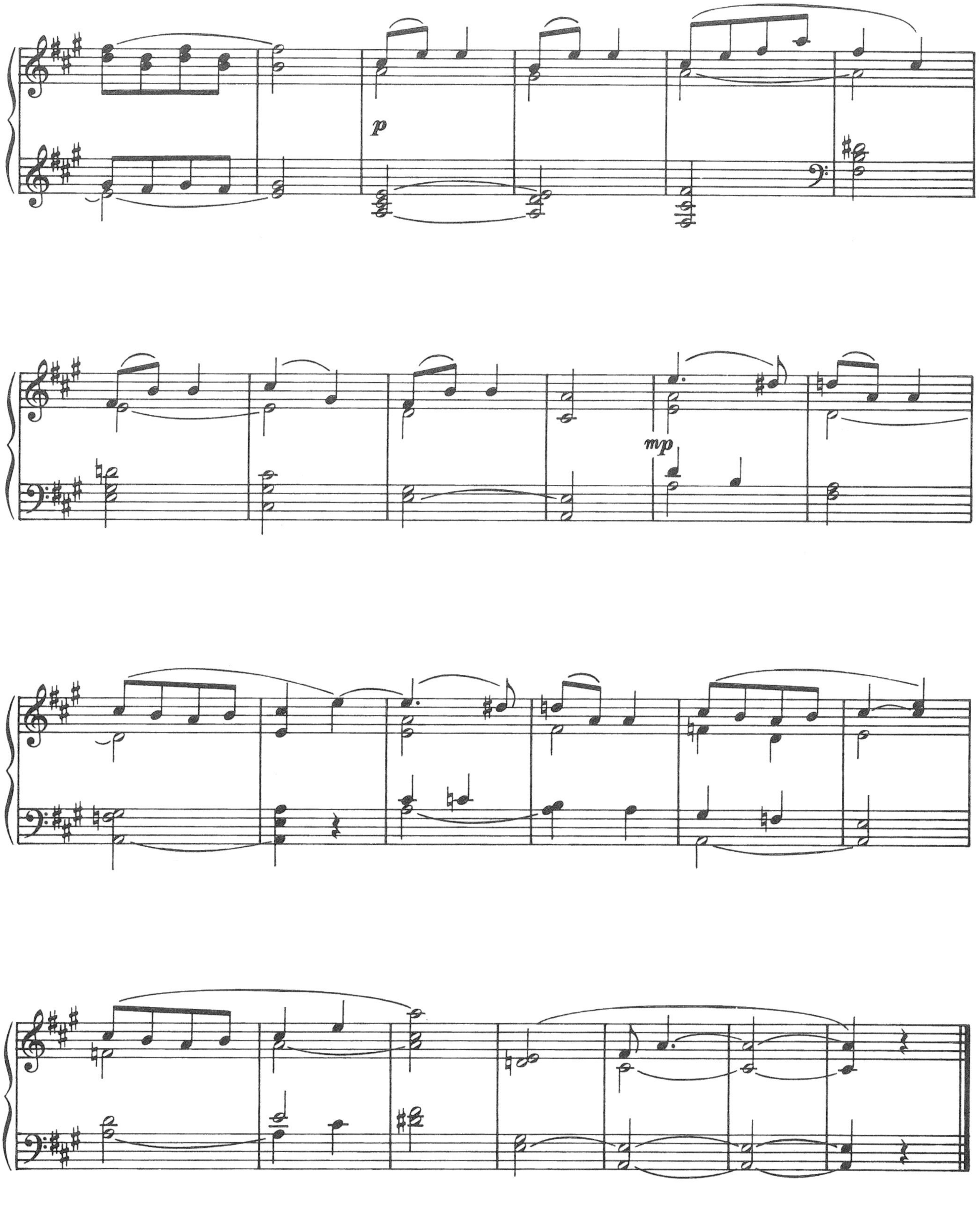
p
mp

A SAD PIECE

Andrew Moore

Lento e espressivo
Sw. 8' Reed

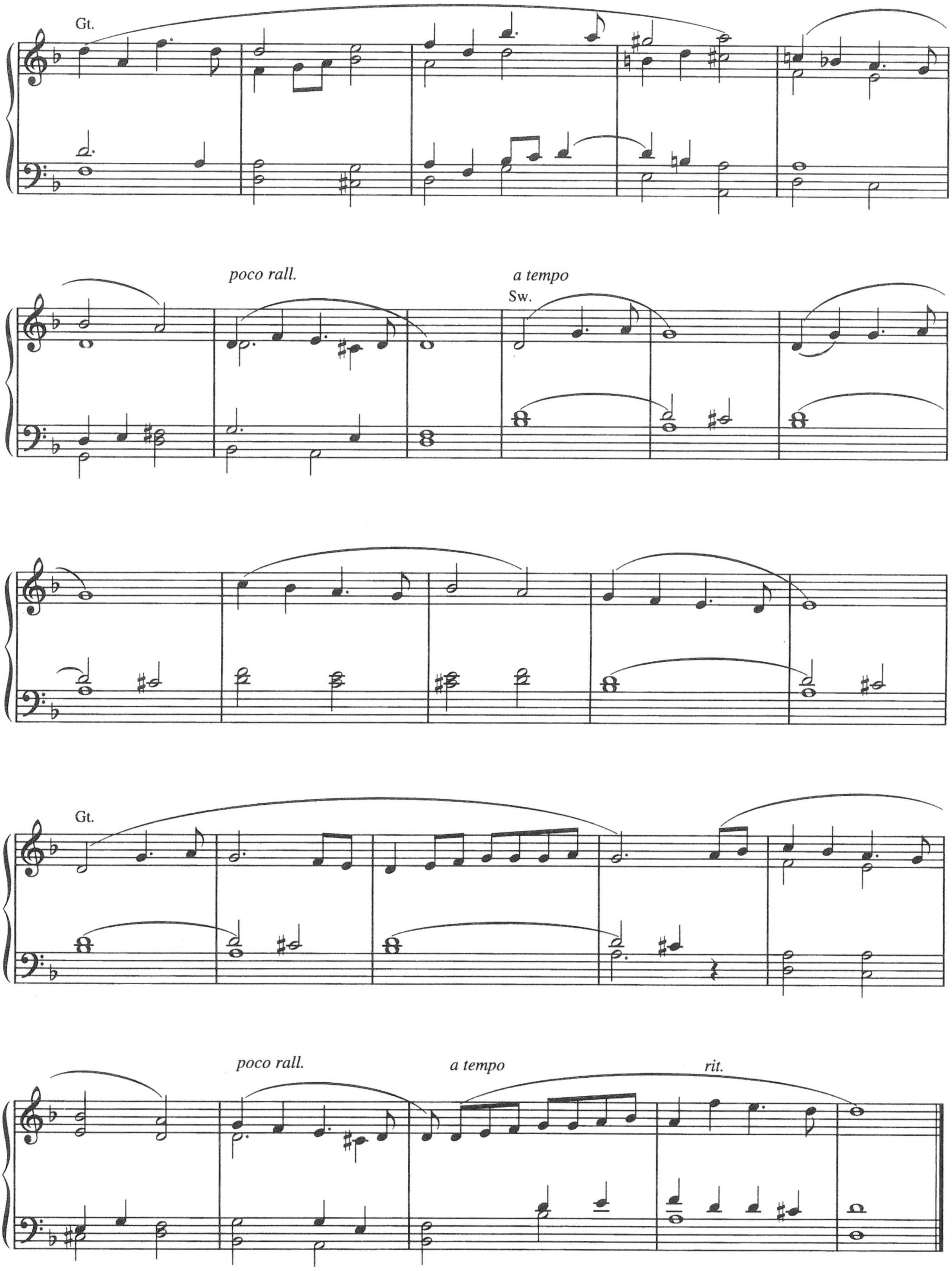
Gt.
poco rall.
a tempo
Sw.
Gt.
poco rall.
a tempo
rit.

REJOICE GREATLY

John Marsh

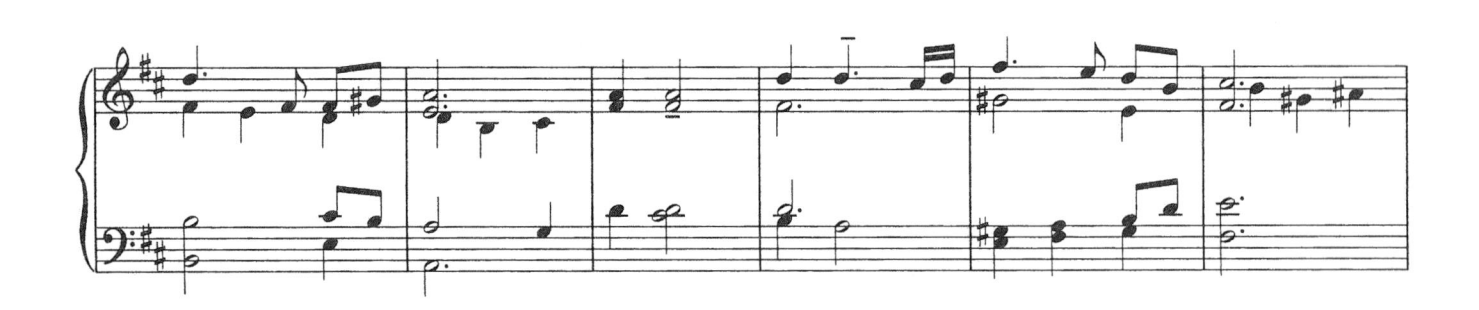

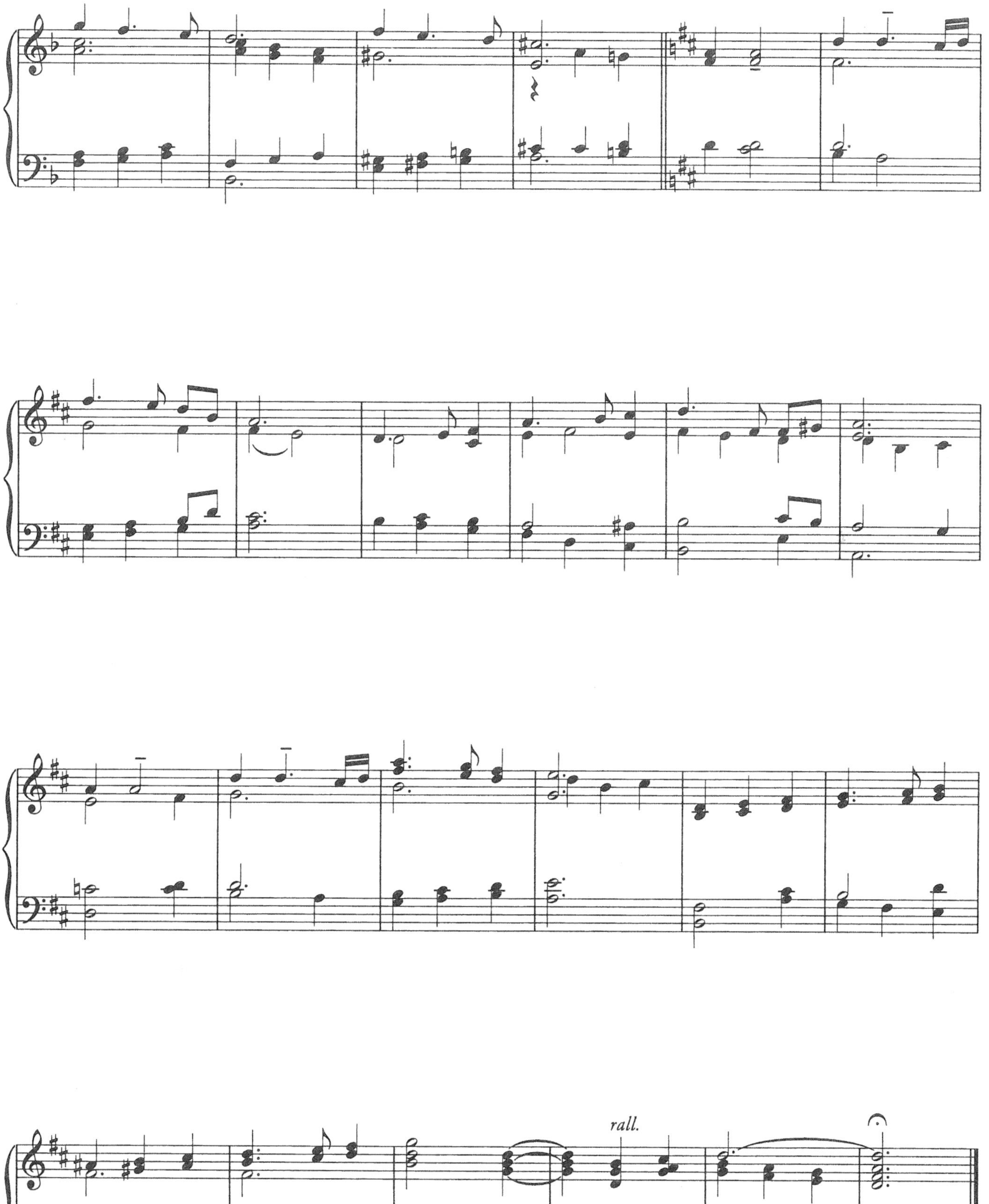
rall.

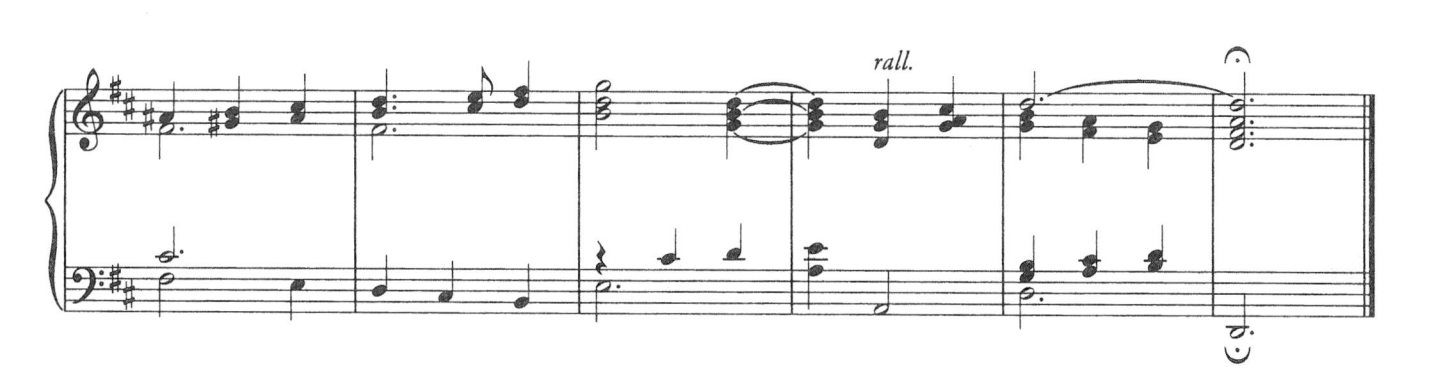

For Brian and Mary

MEDITATION

James Patten

29

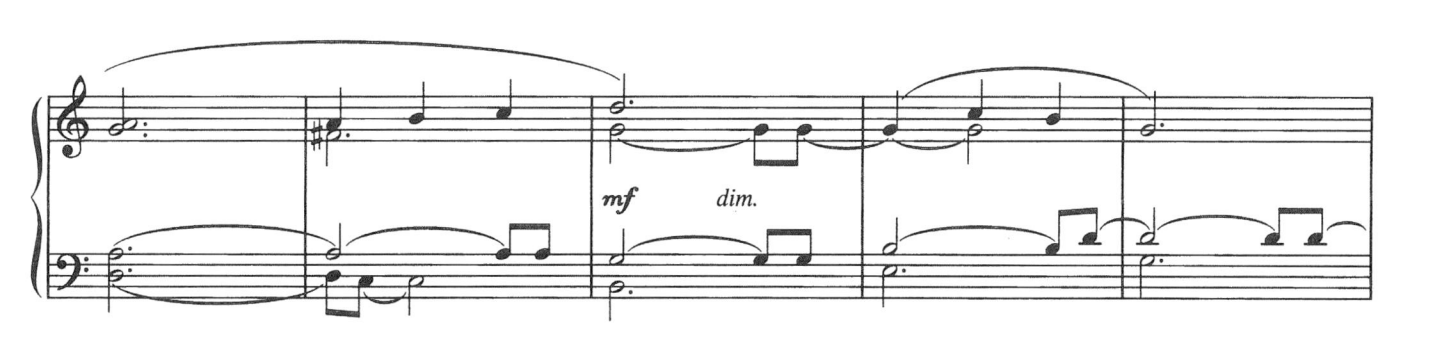

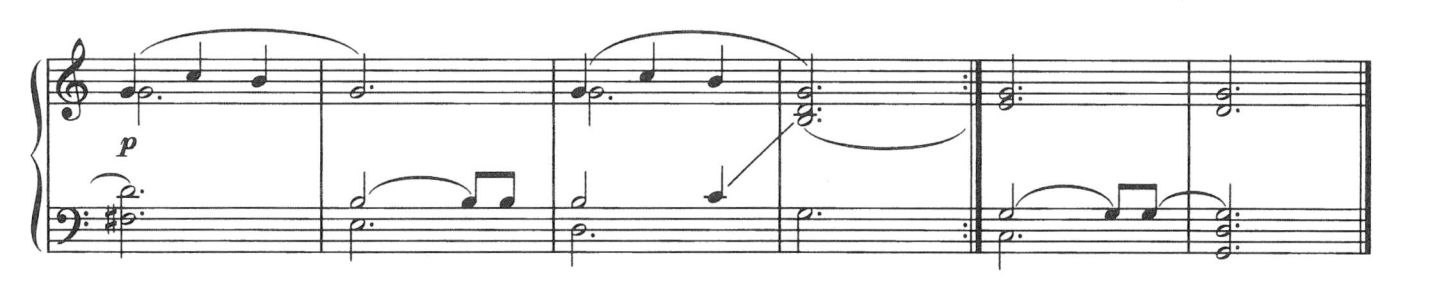

COMMUNION PRELUDE

Michael Higgins

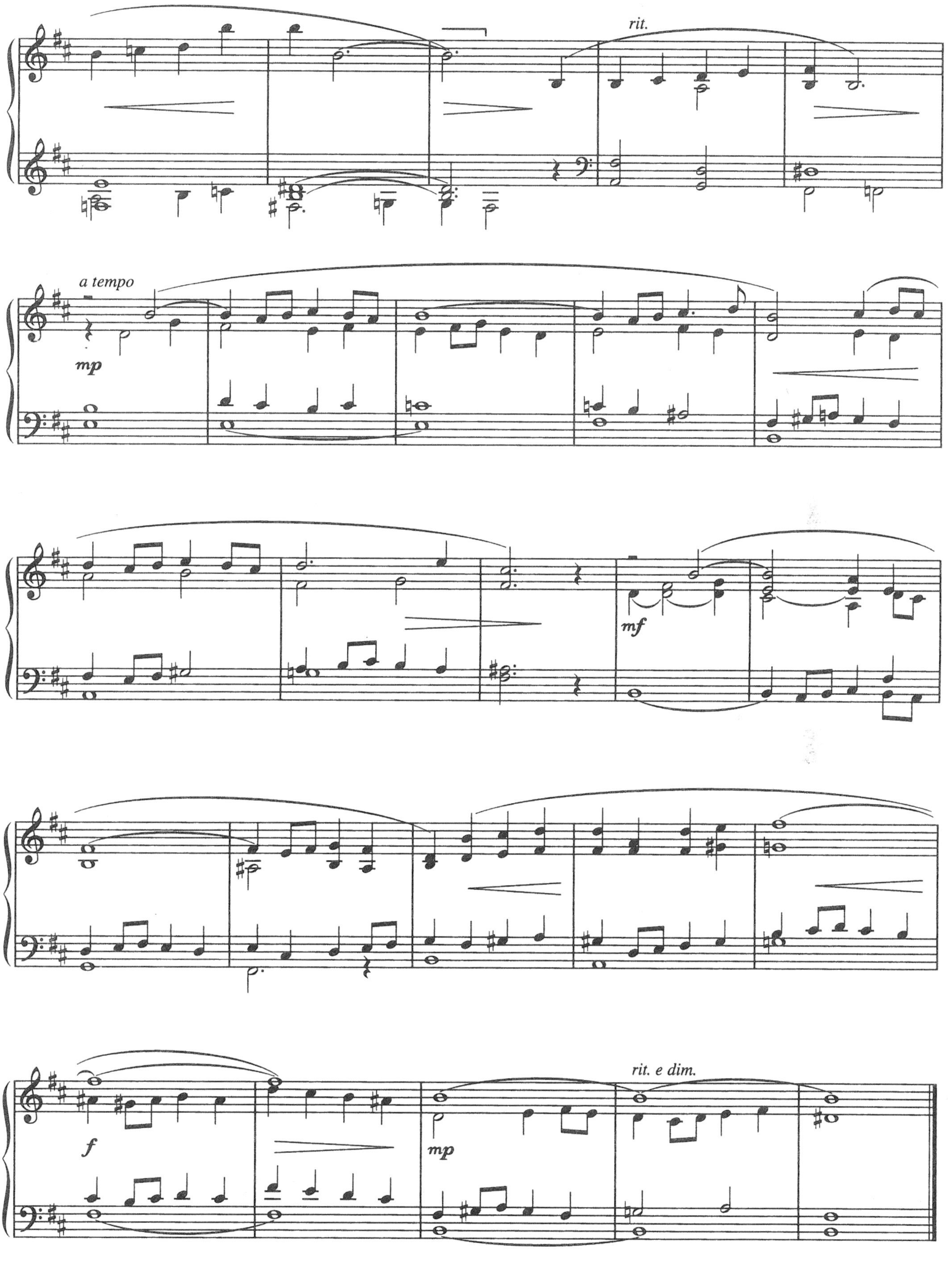
rit.
a tempo
mp
mf
f
mp
rit. e dim.

INVOCATION

Alexandre Guilmant (1837-1911)

33

PRELUDE IN E MINOR

Alexandre Boëly (1785-1858)
arr. Alan Ridout

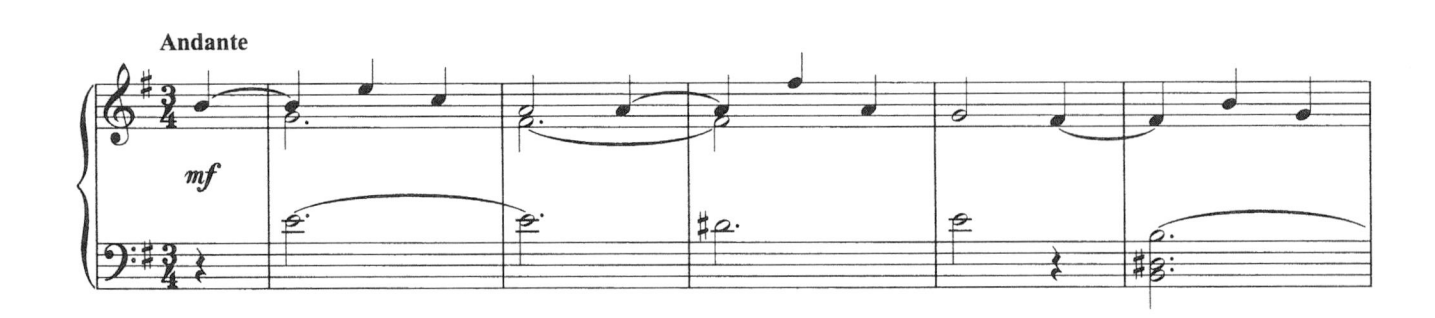

35

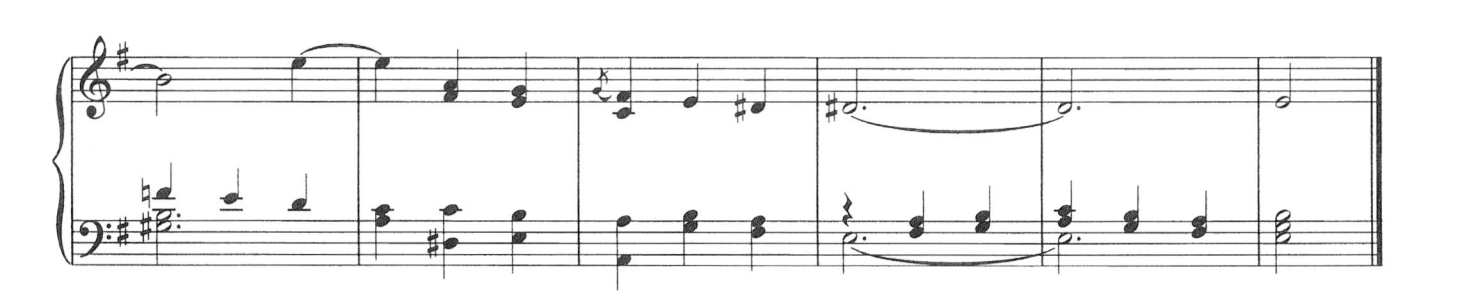

PASTORALE

Elizabeth Hill

Larghetto (♩. = 50)

mp

mf

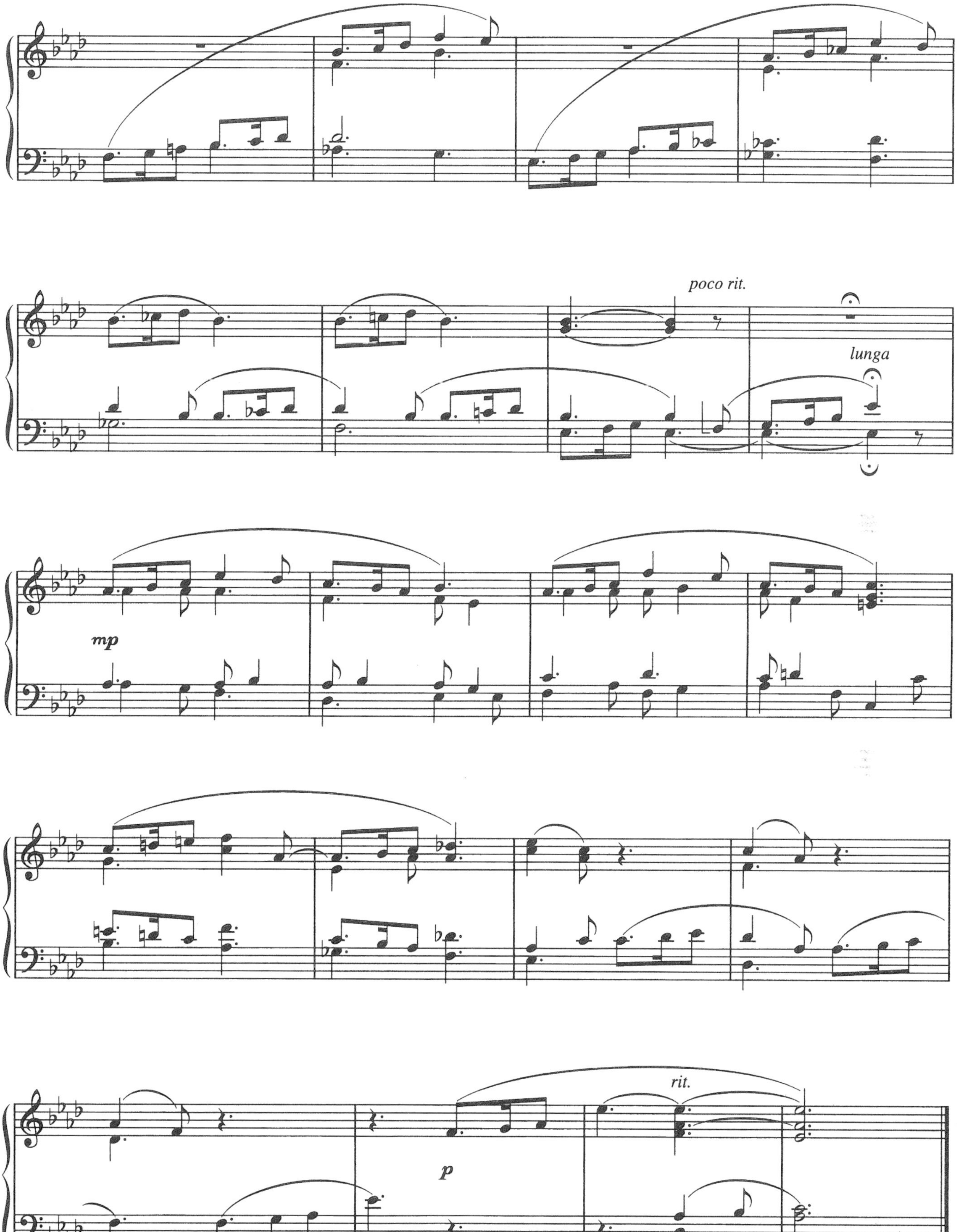
poco rit.
lunga
mp
rit.
p

HAIL THE DAWN
Colin Mawby

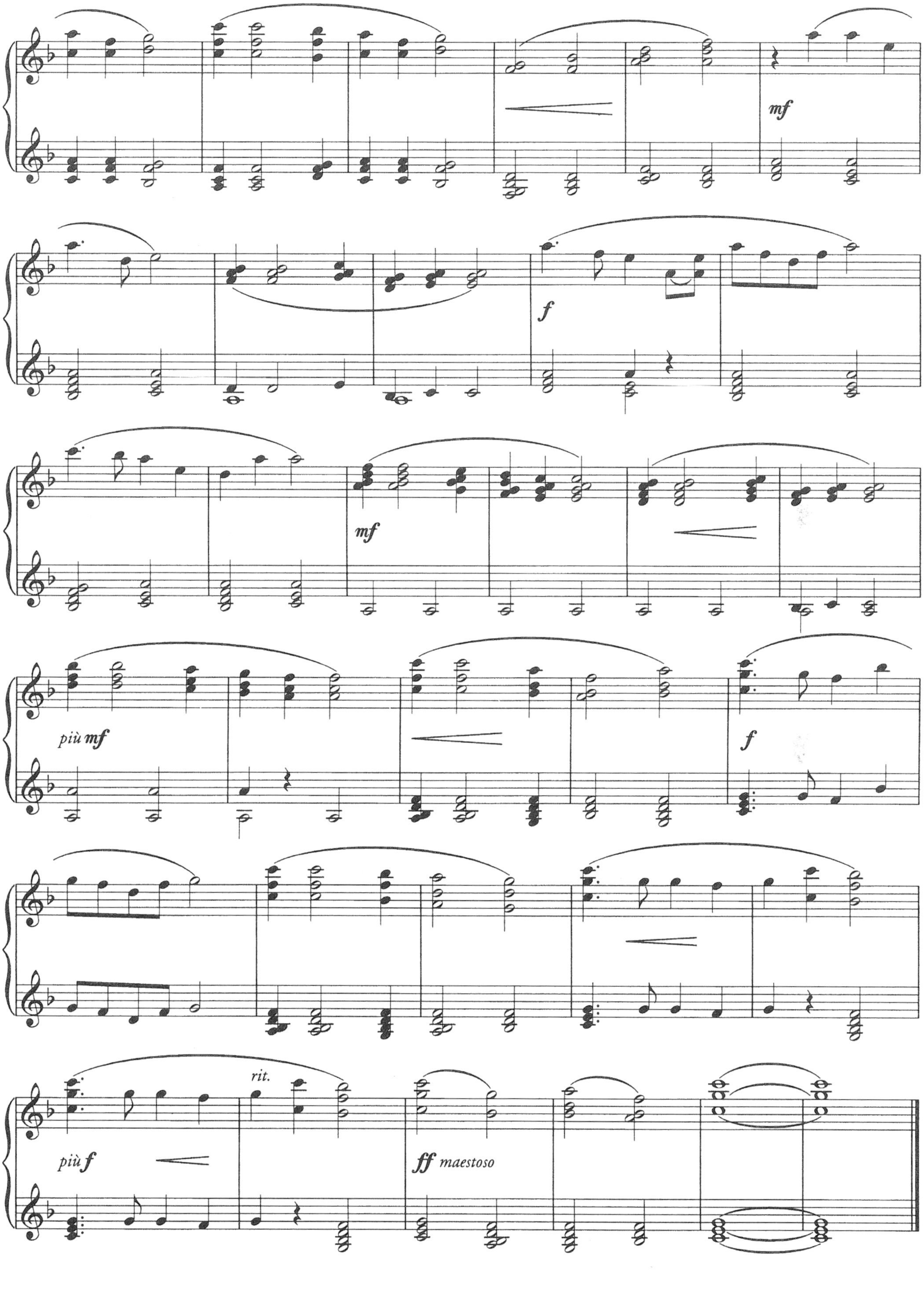
mf
f
mf
più mf
f
più f
rit.
ff maestoso

ANDANTE from SONATINA

Jacob Schmitt (1803-1853)

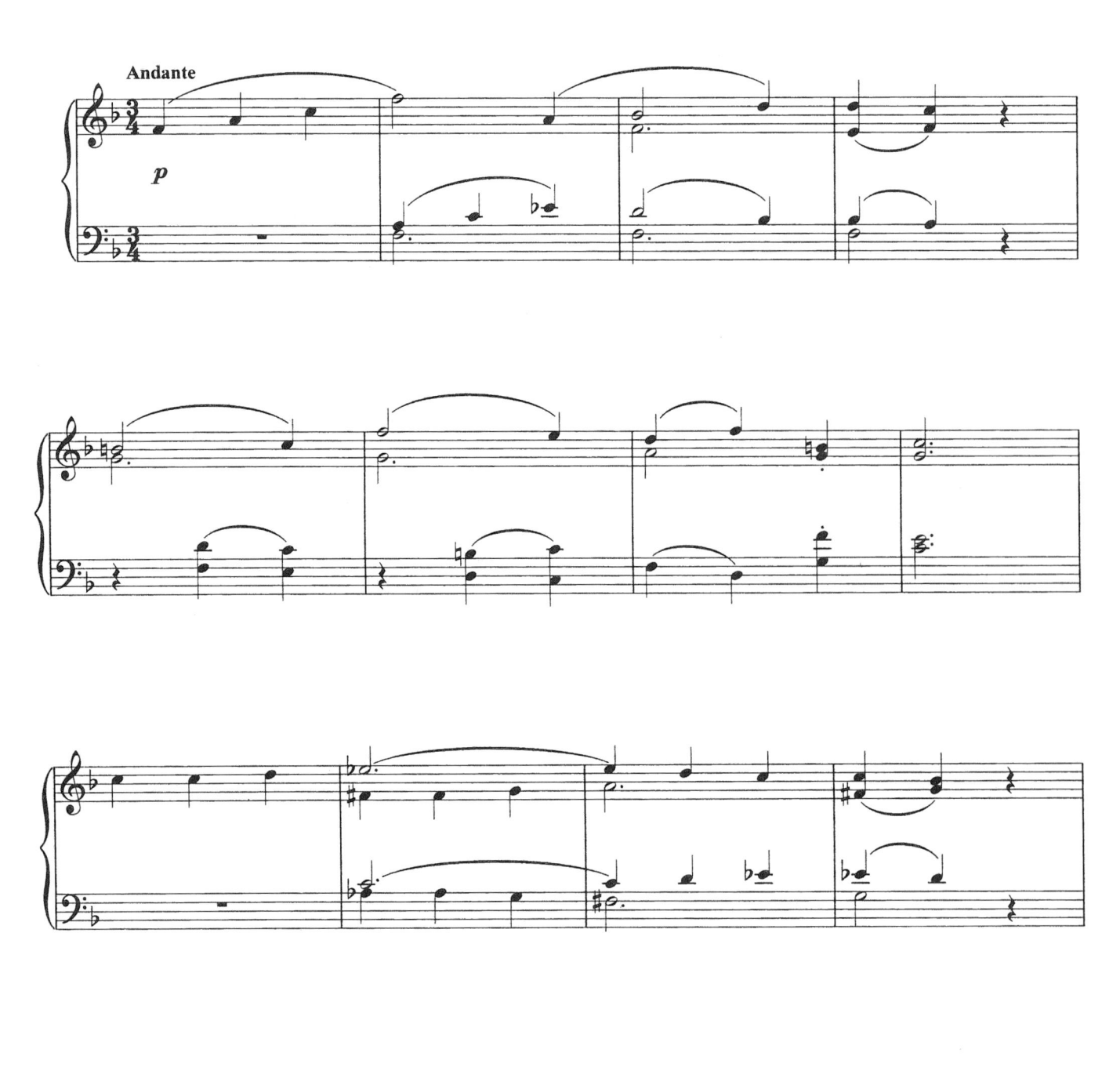

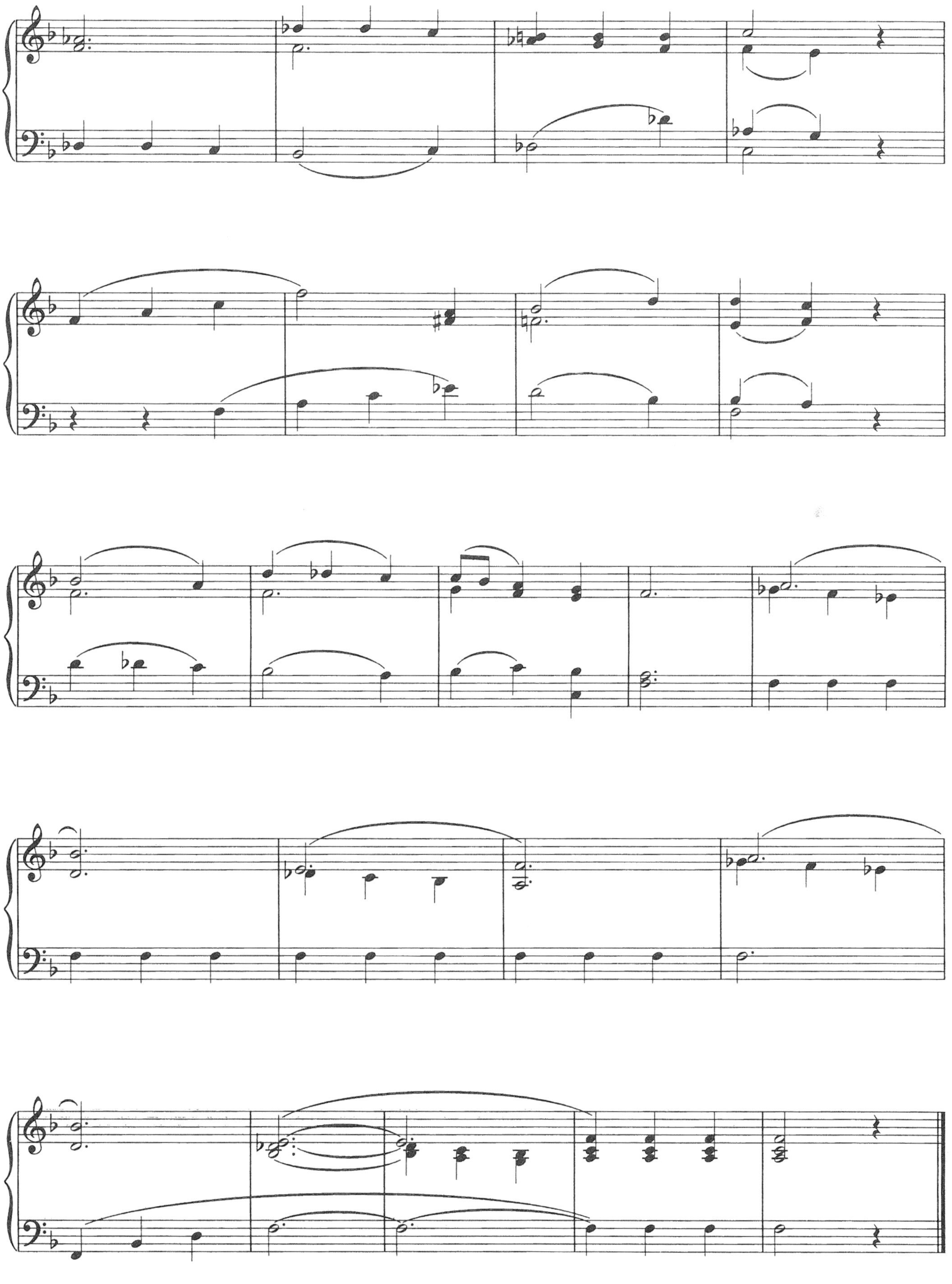

PRELUDE IN C

César Franck (1822-1890)

43

ADAGIO

Christopher Tambling

© Copyright 1993 Kevin Mayhew Ltd.
It is illegal photocopy music.

45

PRELUDE IN B♭

Johann Rinck (1770-1846)

47

FESTAL DAY

Elizabeth Hill

Giocoso (♩ = 130)

ff

mf

f

© Copyright 2000 Kevin Mayhew Ltd.
It is illegal to photocopy music.

2nd time to Coda
cresc.
ff
mf
D.C. al Coda
poco rit.
CODA
rit.
a tempo

DOMINE CLAMAVI

Philip Moore

Andante (♩ = c. 60)

p un poco rubato

© Copyright 1997 Kevin Mayhew Ltd.
It is illegal to photocopy music.

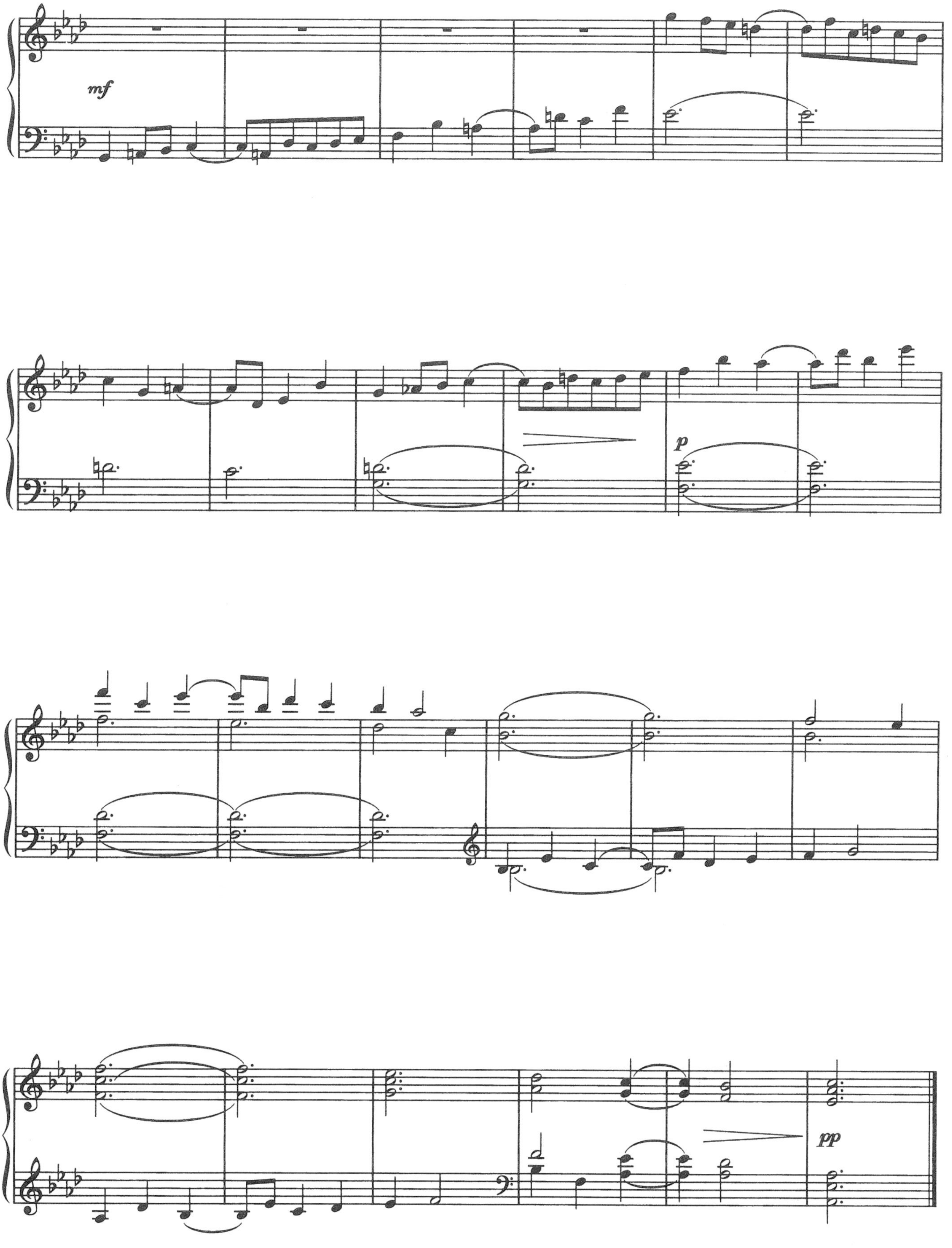
mf
p
pp

OUR LADY'S MORNING SONG

Stanley Vann

*Delicate but bright registration

© Copyright 1997 Kevin Mayhew Ltd.
It is illegal to photocopy music.

53

SLOW AIR

Samuel Wesley (1766-1837)

55

ARIA

Noel Rawsthorne

© Copyright 1993 Kevin Mayhew Ltd.
It is illegal photocopy music.

cresc. poco a poco
mf
dim. poco a poco
poco rall.
ten.
p
ten.
Tempo I
Gt.
mp
Sw.
poco a poco rall. al fine

A PRAYER SONG

Andrew Moore

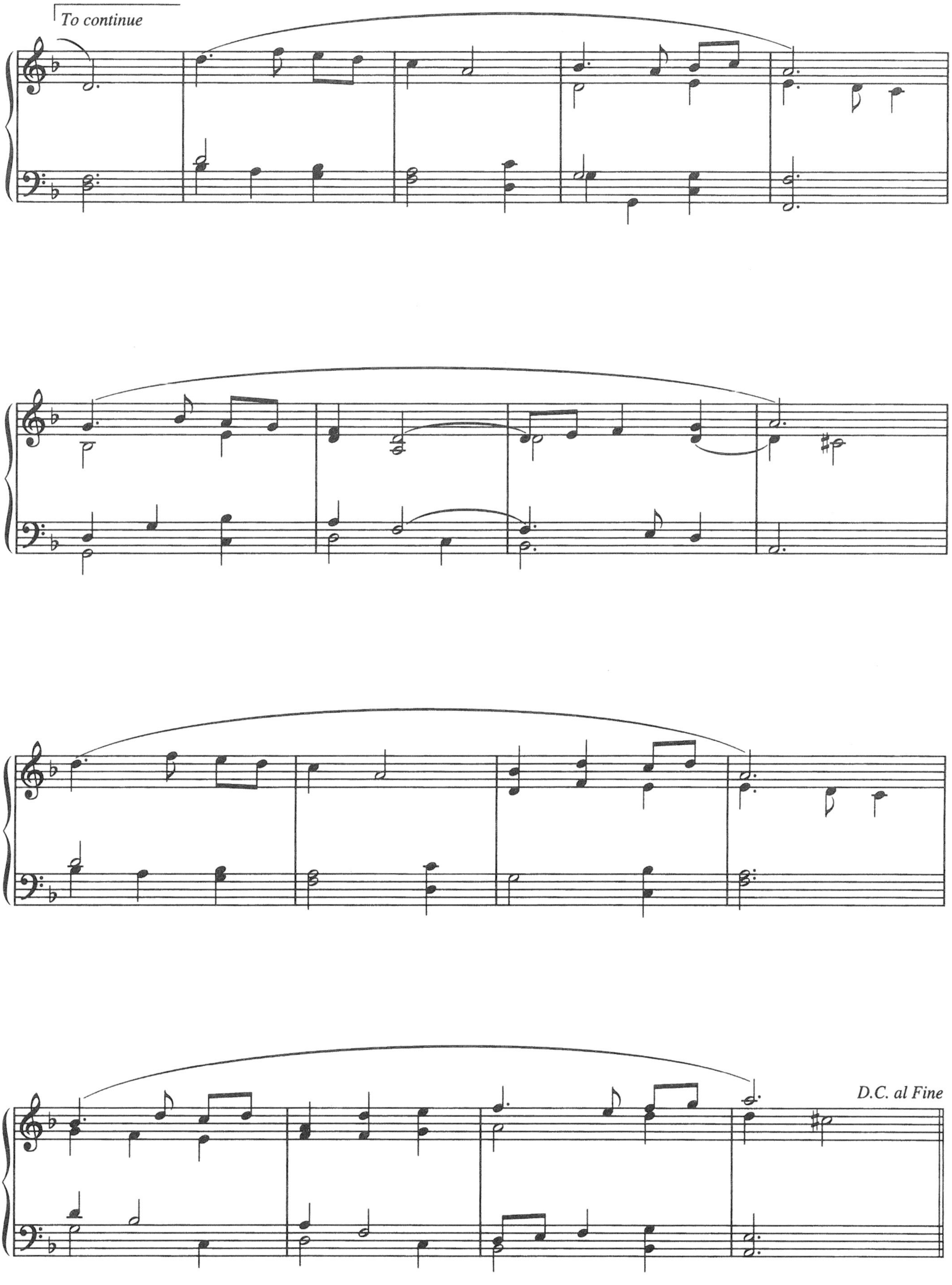
To continue
D.C. al Fine

MALLABY-DEELEY'S MARCH

Richard Lloyd

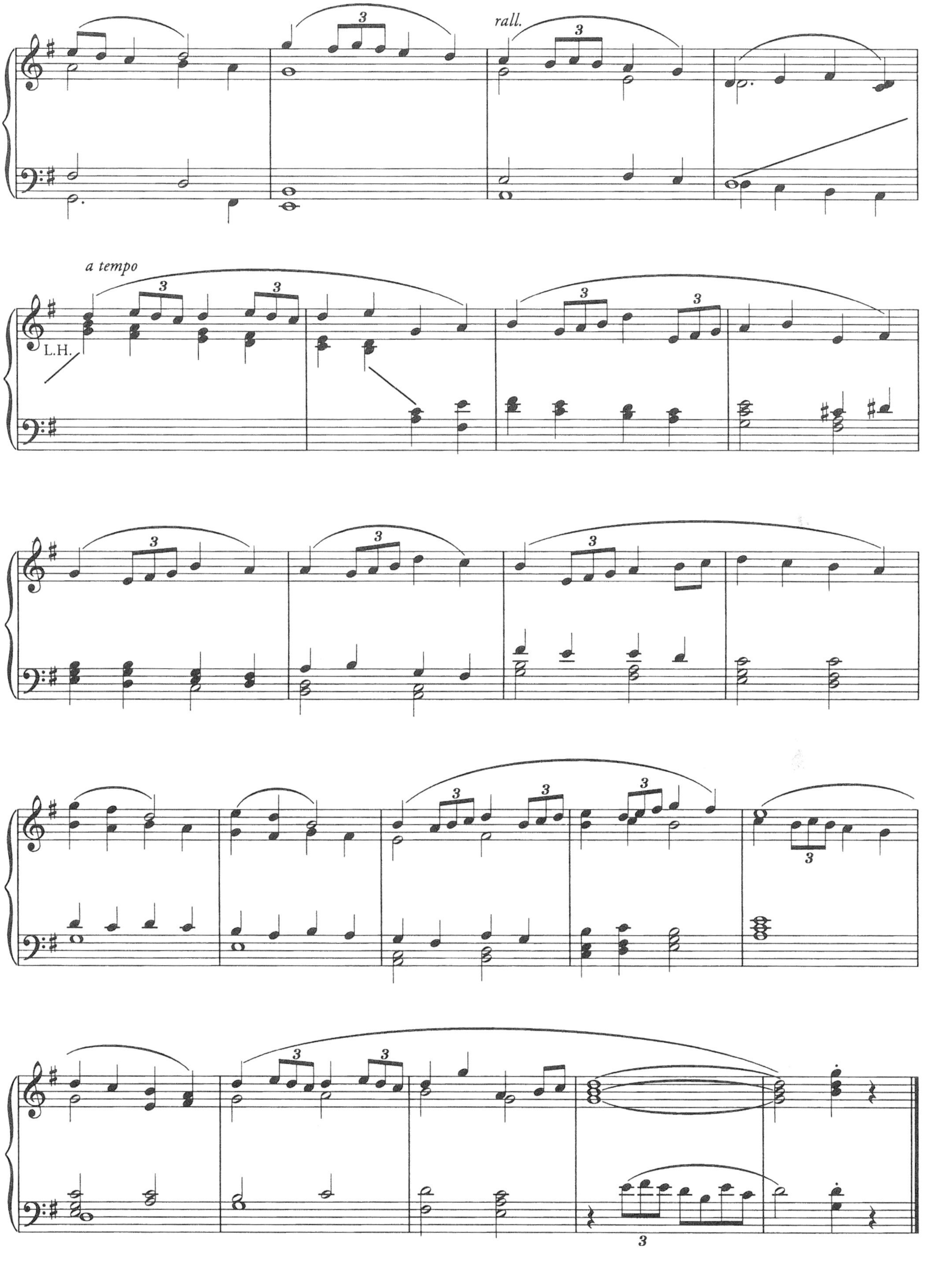
rall.
a tempo
L.H.

PROCESSION TO A JAUNTY TUNE

Rosalie Bonighton

© Copyright 1999 Kevin Mayhew Ltd.
It is illegal to photocopy music.

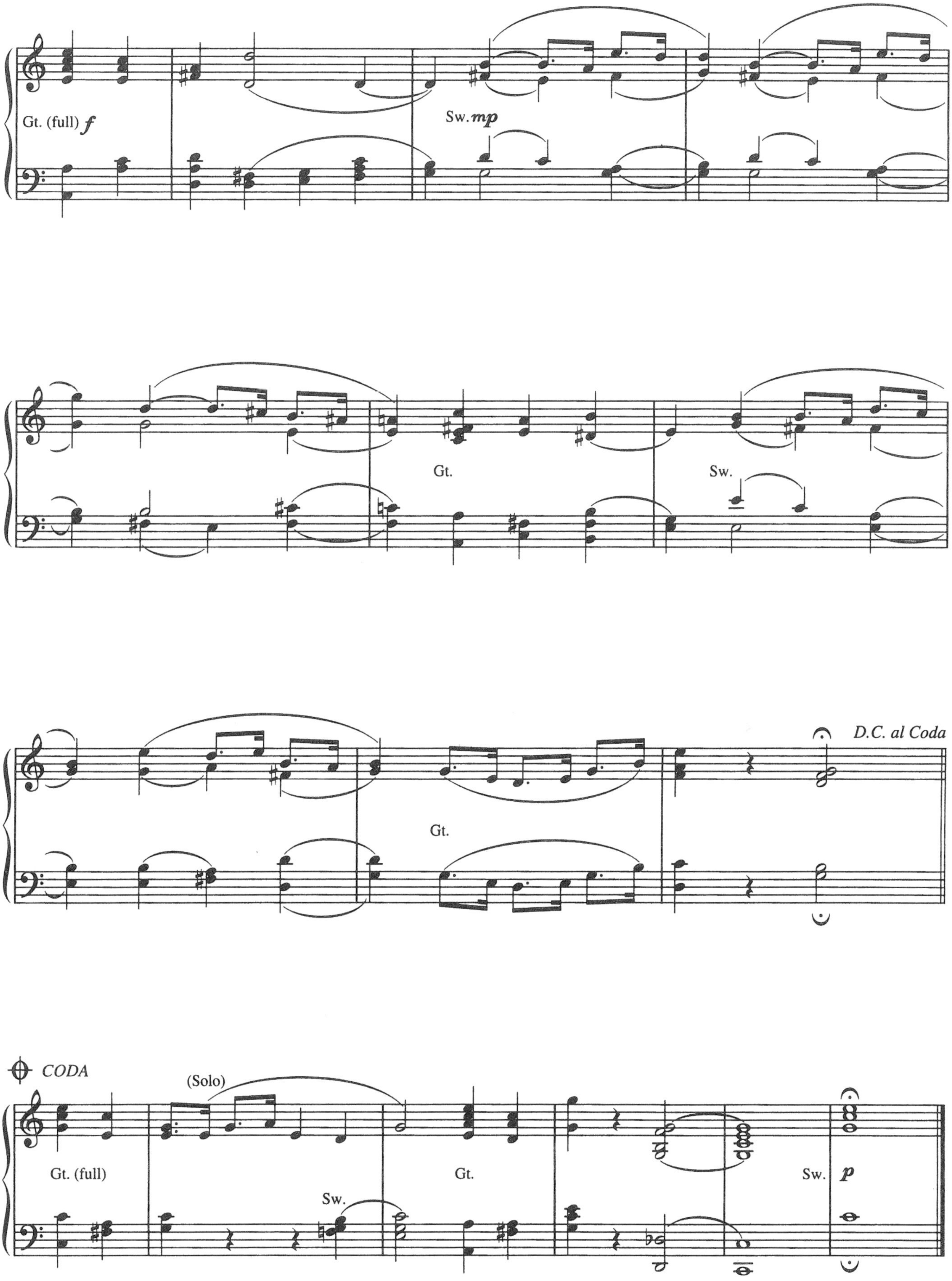
Gt. (full) f
Sw. mp
Gt.
Sw.
Gt.
D.C. al Coda
CODA
(Solo)
Gt. (full)
Sw.
Gt.
Sw. p

For Peter and Emma

MEDITATION AT ENGELBERG

John Marsh

65

PRELUDE

Gustav Merkel (1827-1885)

IMPROVISATION

Andrew Moore (b.1954)

VOLUNTARY

William Croft (1678-1727)

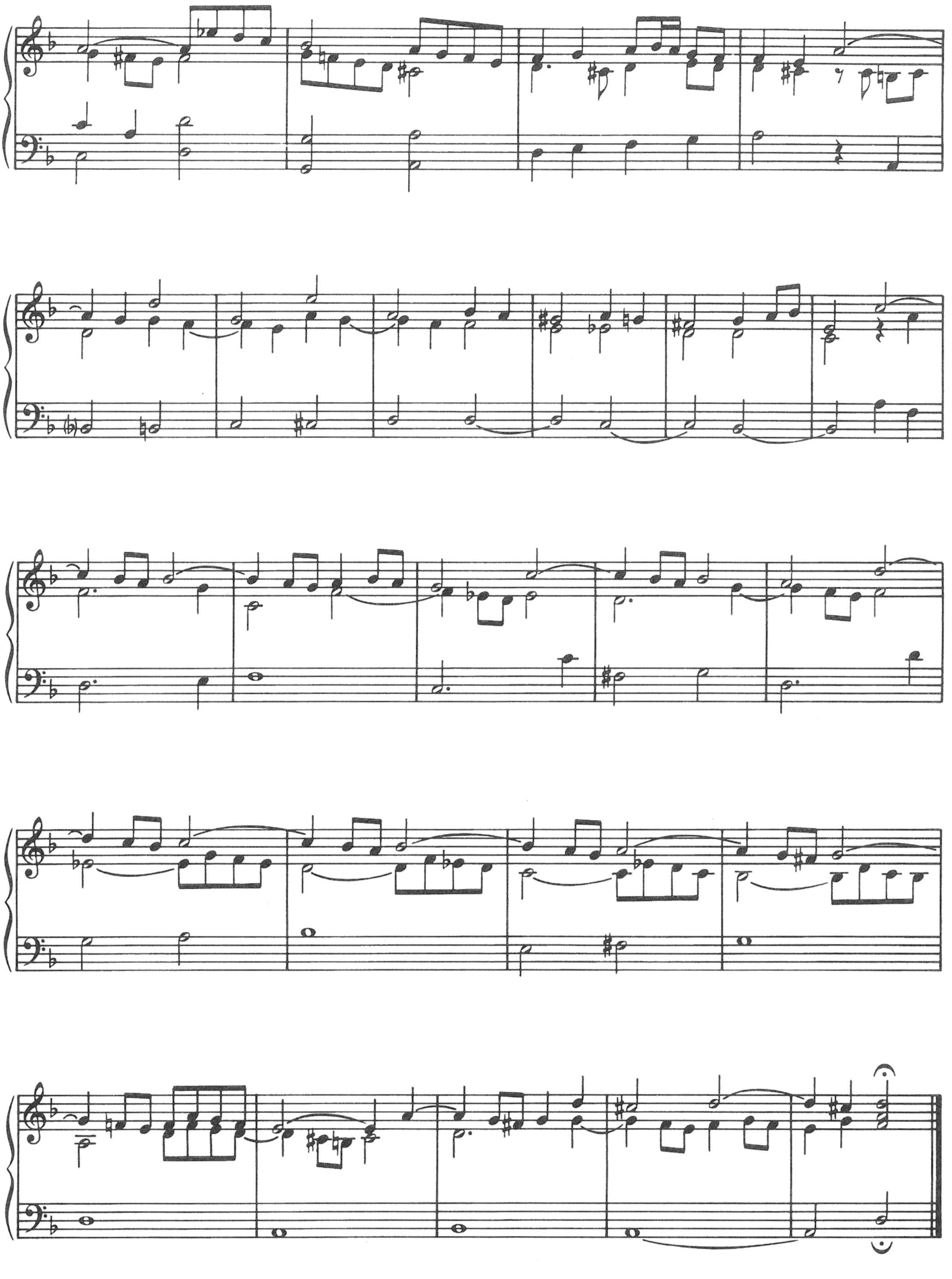

CHANT DE MATIN

Léon Boëllmann (1862-1897)
arr. Alan Ridout

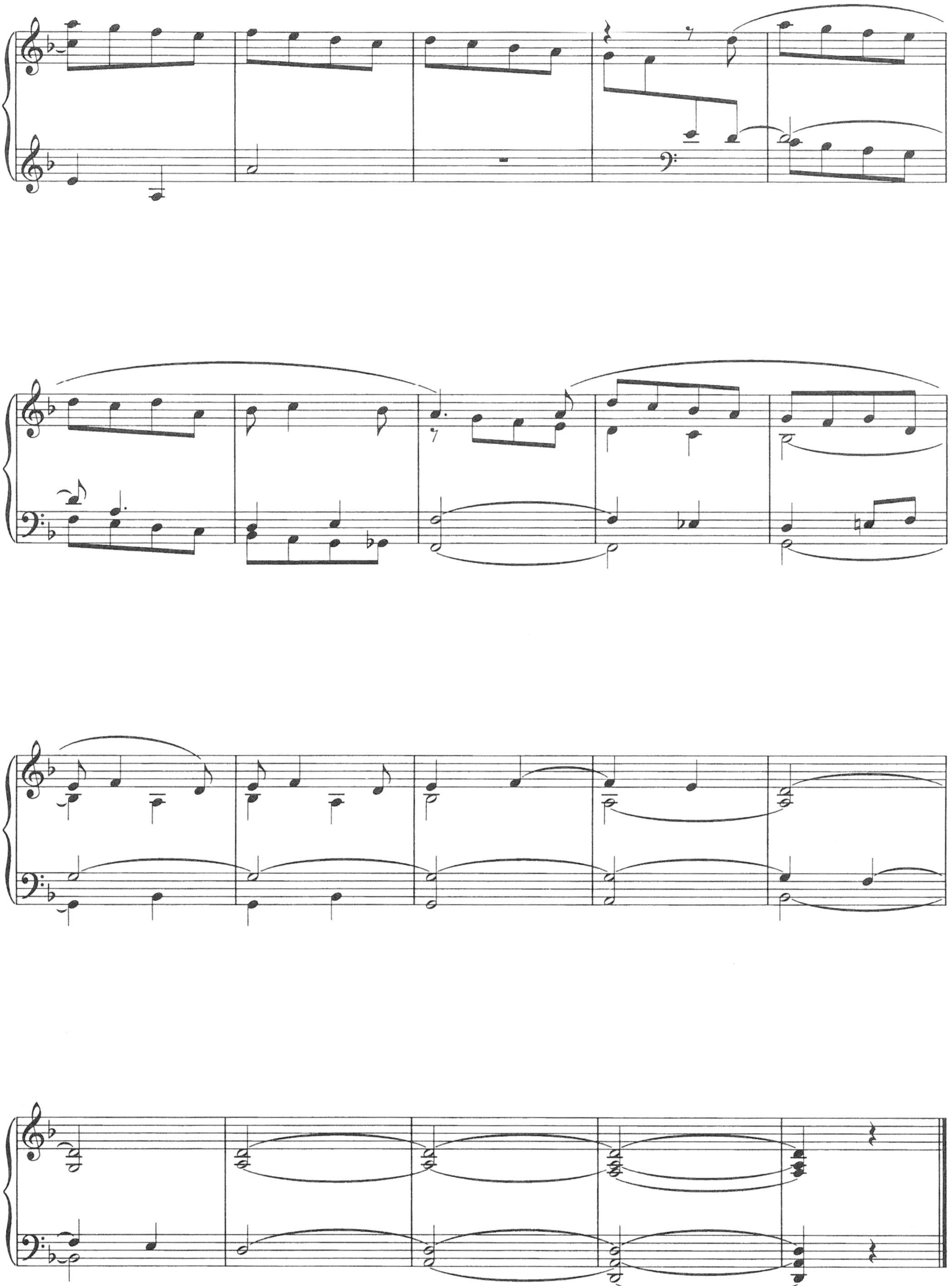

ANDANTINO

César Franck (1822-1890)

73

For Dom Cyprian Stockford

NOBILMENTE

Andrew Moore

© Copyright 1993 Kevin Mayhew Ltd.
It is illegal photocopy music.

75

ARIA

Richard Lloyd

77

PRIERE

César Franck (1822-1890)

PRAYER TO THE TRINITY

Andrew Moore

ARIETTA

John Marsh

Adagio
Solo Flute or Oboe 8'

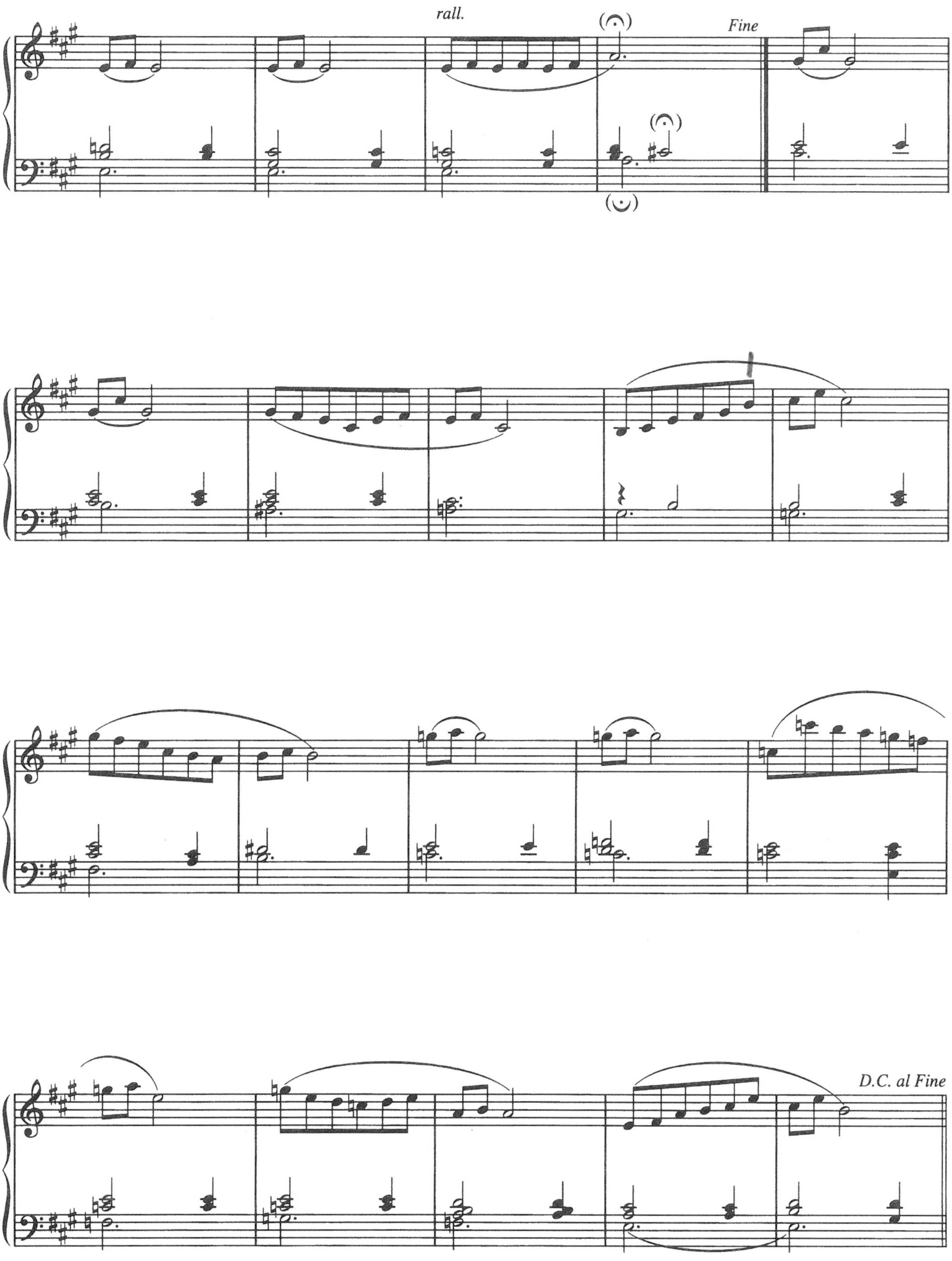
rall.
Fine
D.C. al Fine

ANDANTE TRANQUILLO

Gregory Murray (1905-1992)

© Copyright 1993 Kevin Mayhew Ltd.
It is illegal photocopy music.

83

PASTORALE

Léon Boëllmann (1862-1897)

PRELUDE IN C

Carl Nielson (1865-1931)

CRADLE SONG

Richard Lloyd

Tempo comodo

pp

© Copyright 2000 Kevin Mayhew Ltd.
It is illegal to photocopy music.

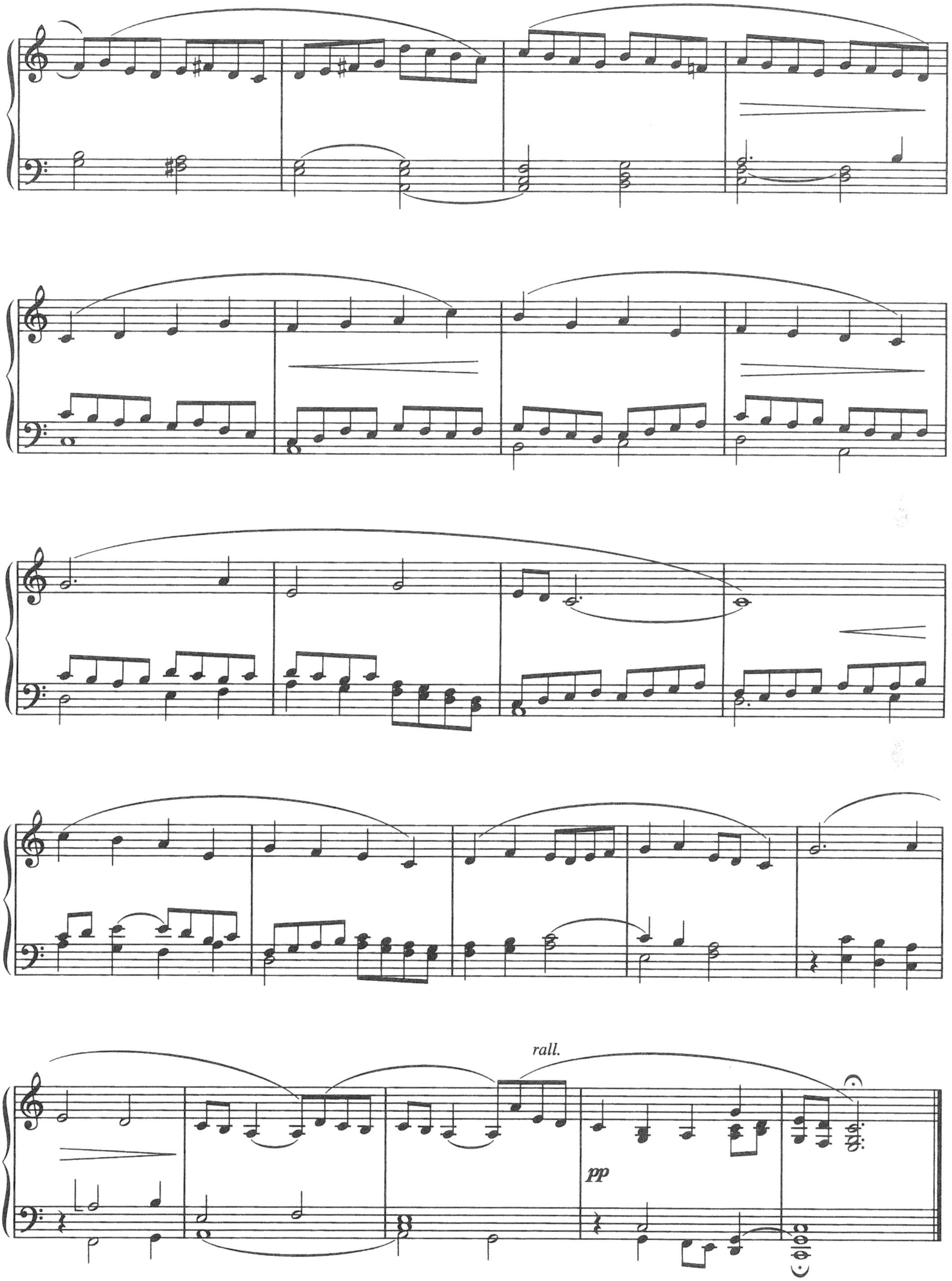
rall.
pp

LA FURSTEMBERG

Michel Corrette (1709-1795)

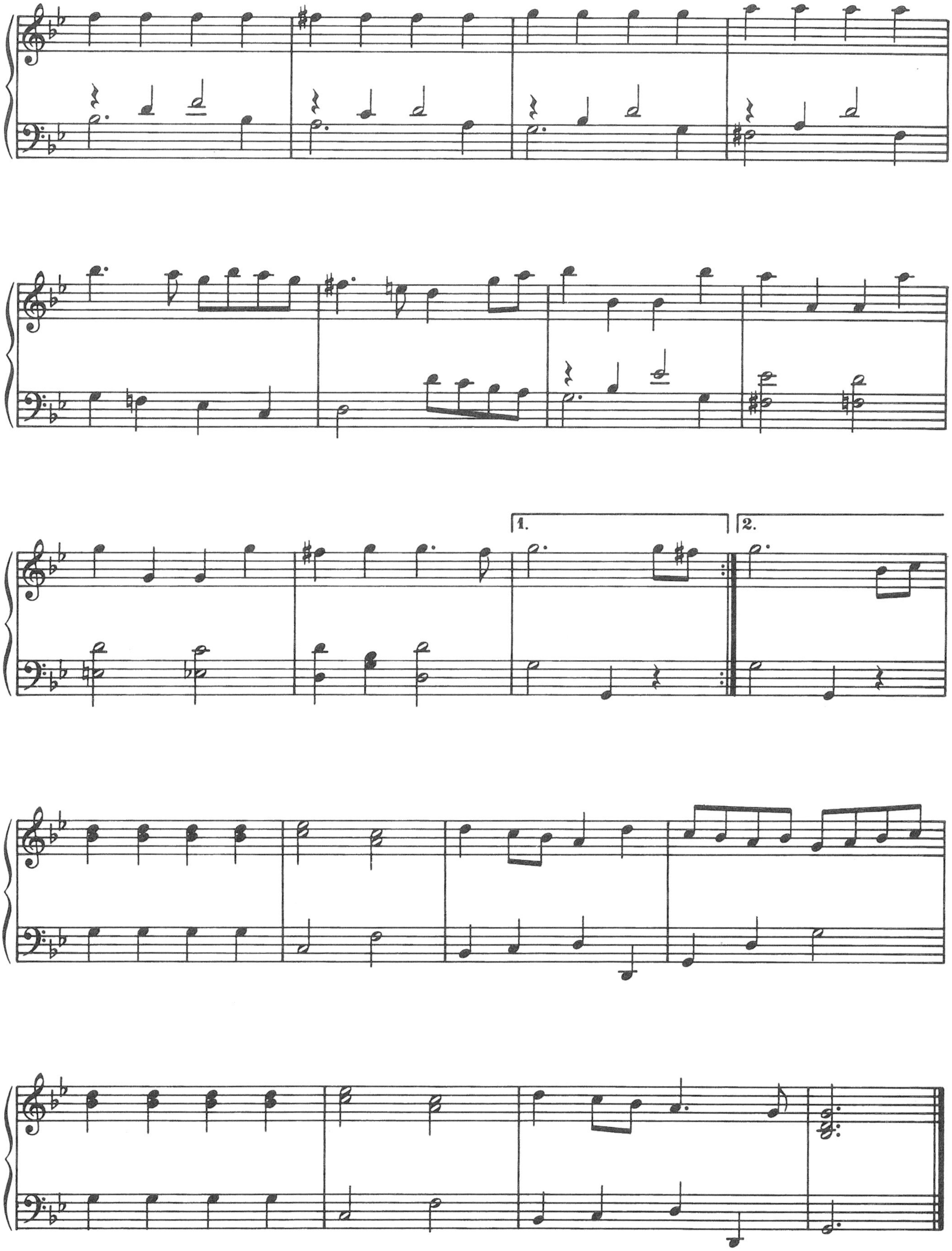
1.
2.

For Peter Matthews

A TUBA MINUET

Christopher Tambling

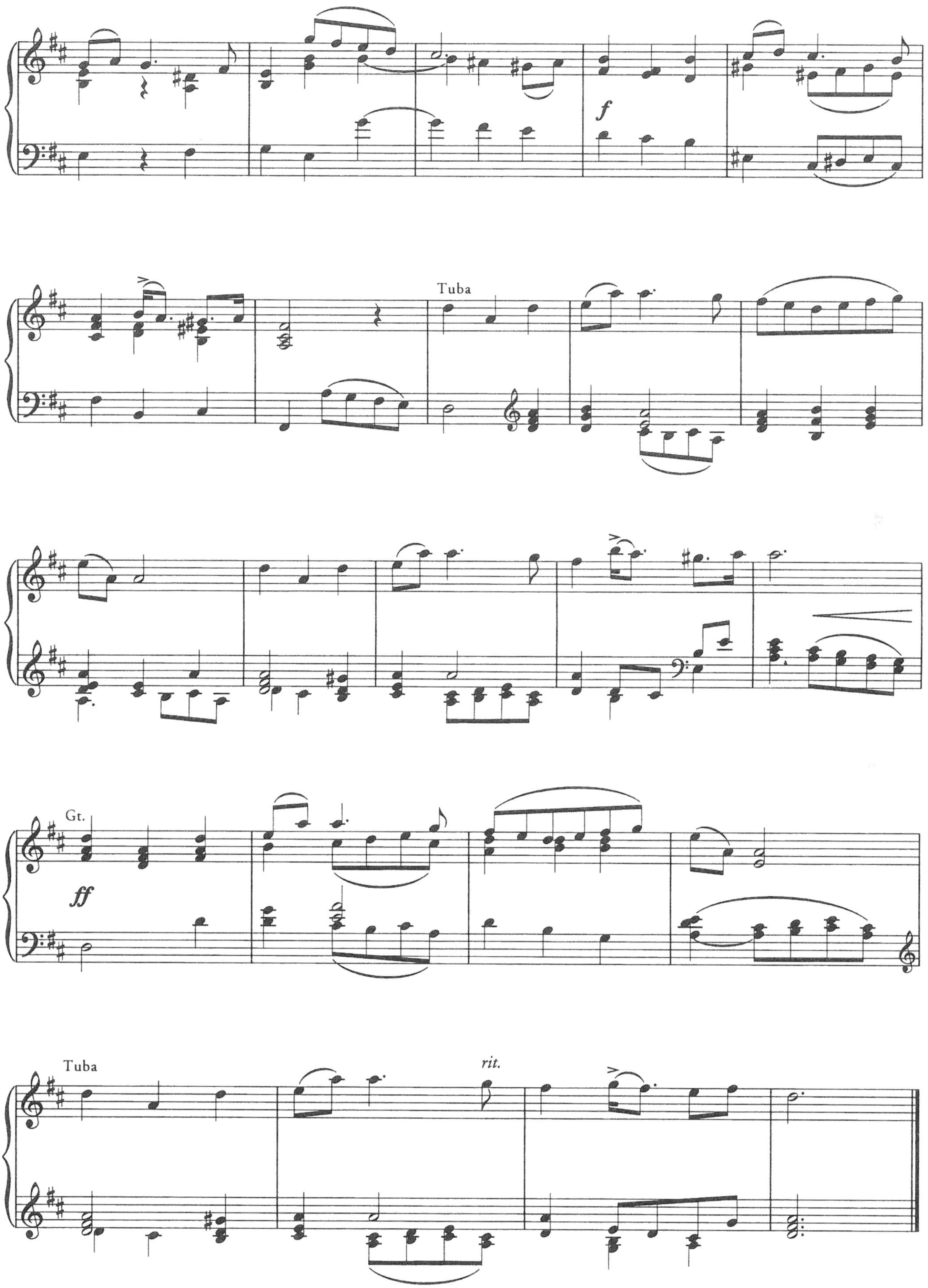
f
Tuba
Gt.
ff
Tuba
rit.

PROMENADE

June Nixon

93

PRELUDE IN D MINOR

Anton Bruckner (1824-1896)

STROPHE

Alexandre Guilmant (1837-1911)

IDYLL

Edward MacDowell (1860-1908)

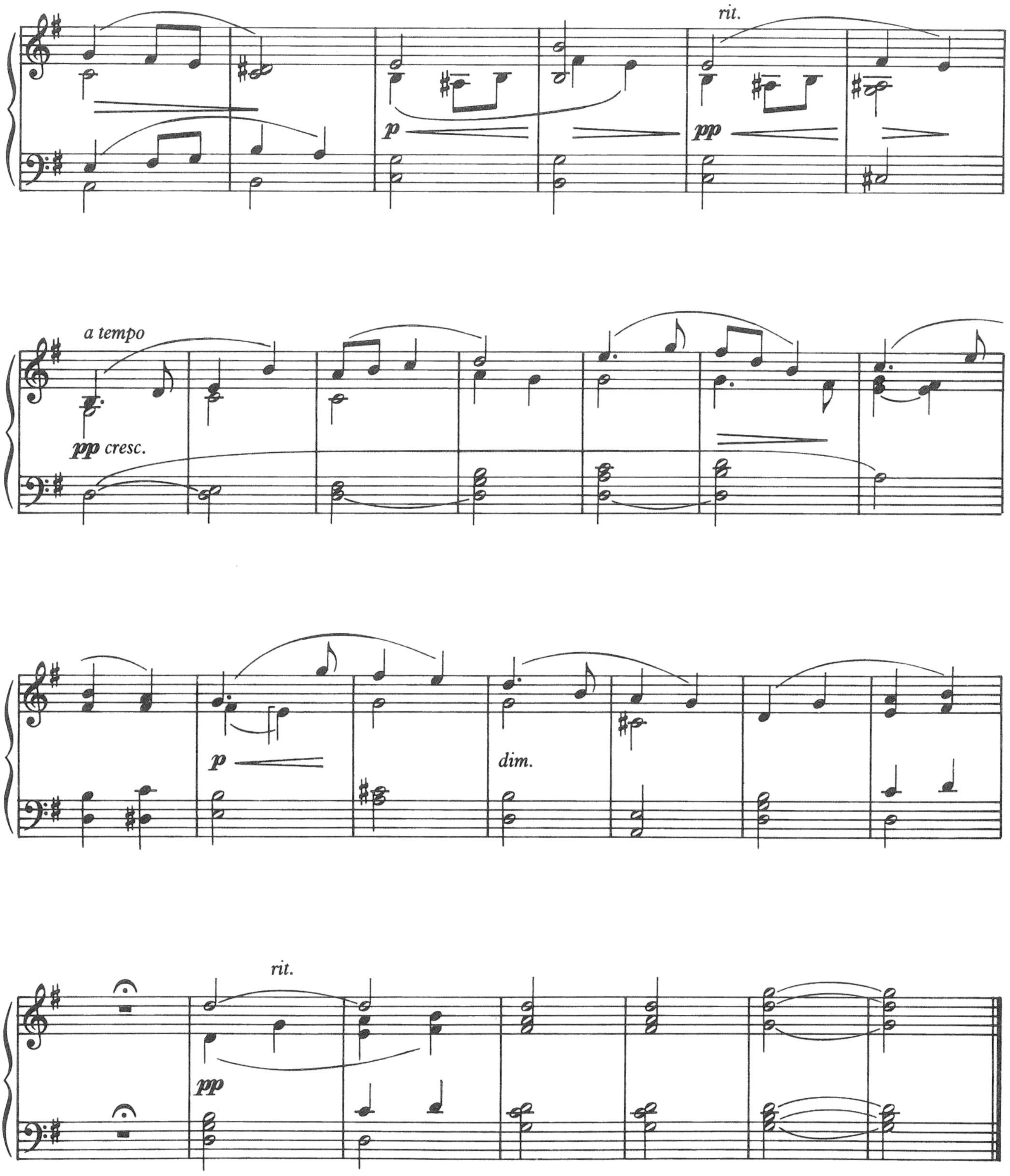
rit.
p
pp
a tempo
pp cresc.
p
dim.
rit.
pp

A PRAYER OF PEACE

"Lord, help me to treasure stillness and rest, for therein lies your strength."
Based on Isaiah 30:15

Michael Higgins

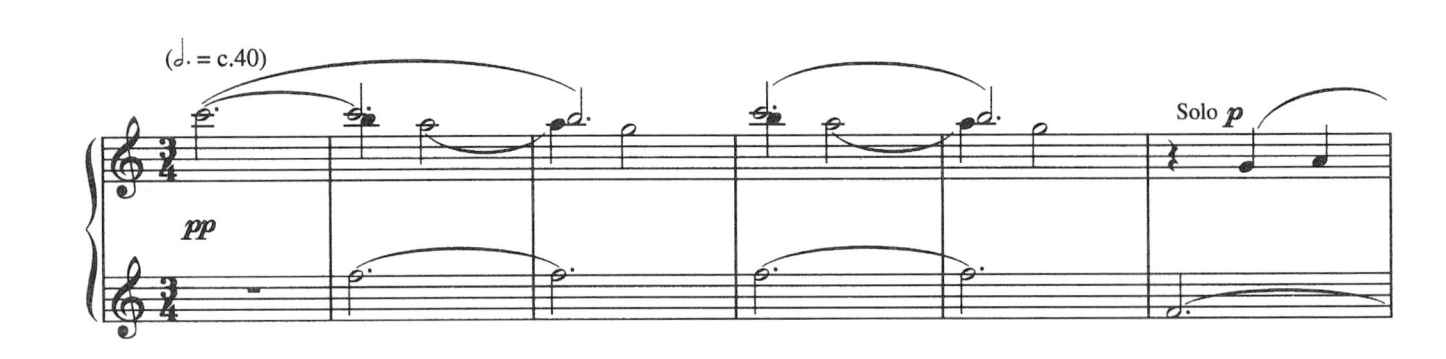

99

ARIOSO

Noel Rawsthorne

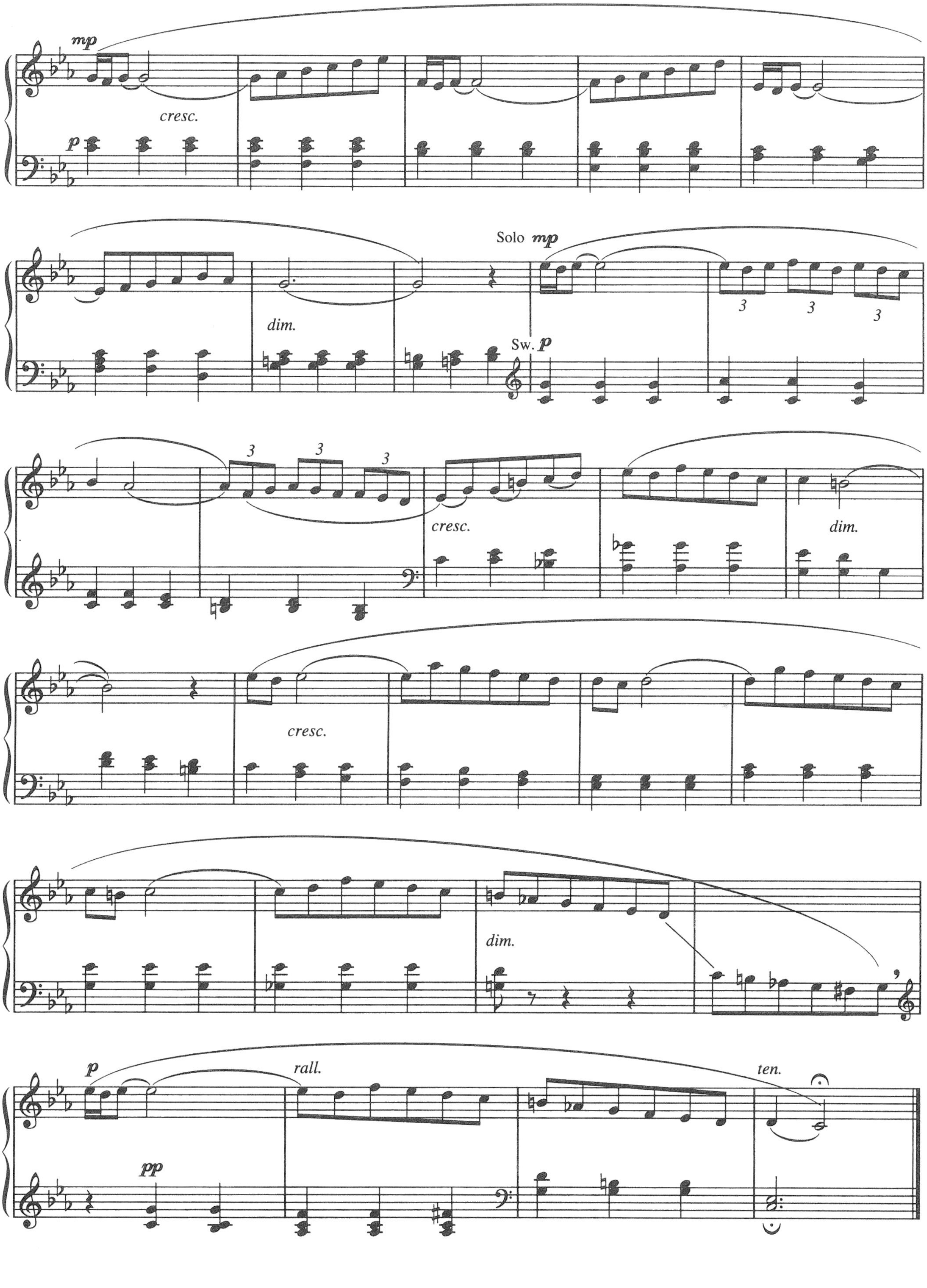
mp
p
cresc.
dim.
Solo mp
Sw. p
cresc.
dim.
cresc.
dim.
p
rall.
ten.
pp

PRELUDE

Zděnek Fibich (1850-1900)
arr. Alan Ridout

ANDANTE

Johann Rinck (1770-1846)

For Sheila

COUNTRY MINUET

Graham Knott

© Copyright 1993 Kevin Mayhew Ltd.
It is illegal photocopy music.

INTERLUDE

Noel Rawsthorne

© Copyright 1993 Kevin Mayhew Ltd.
It is illegal photocopy music.

TRUMPET TUNE

David Terry

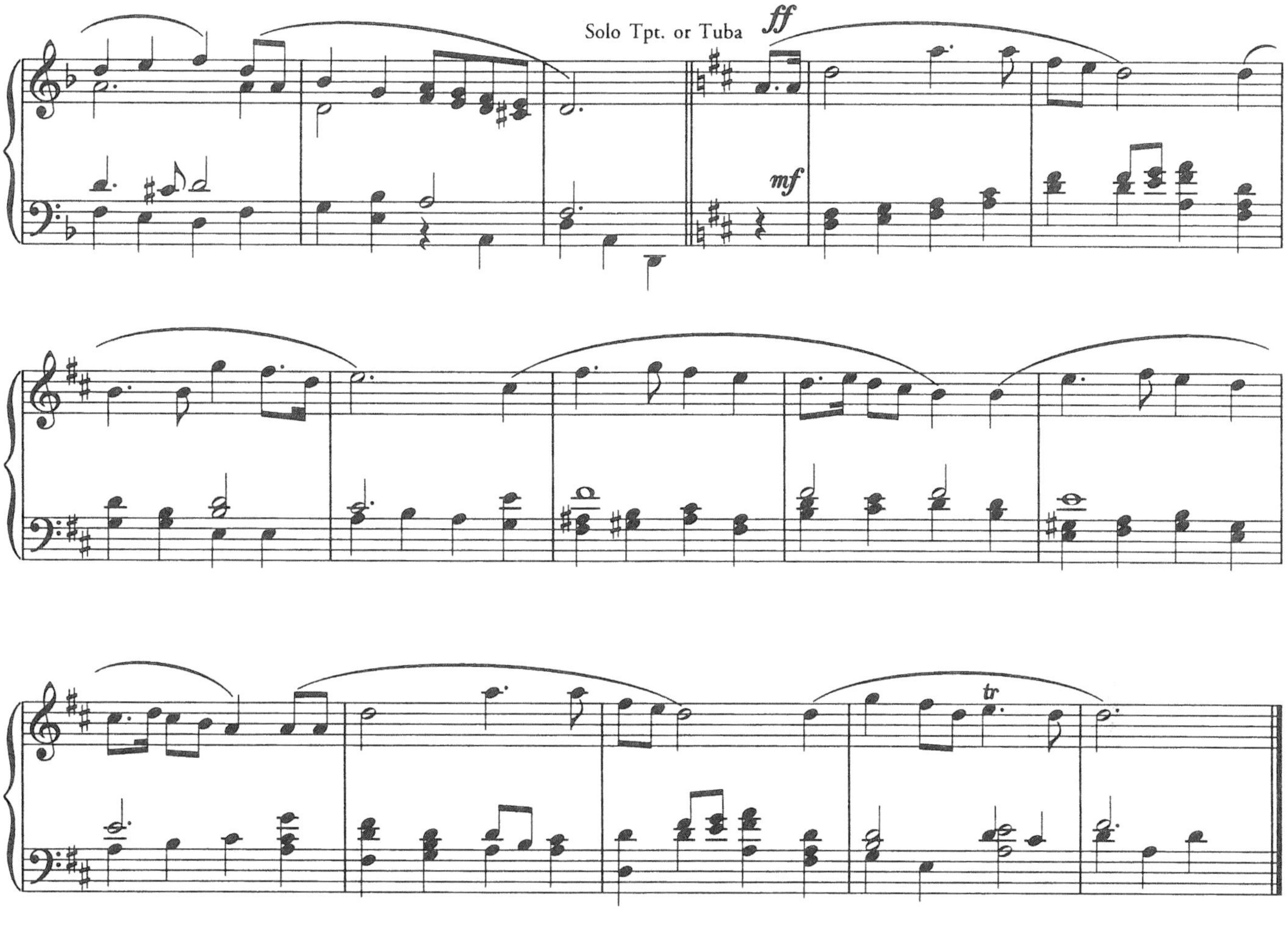
Solo Tpt. or Tuba
ff
mf
tr

CANTABILE

Simon Clark

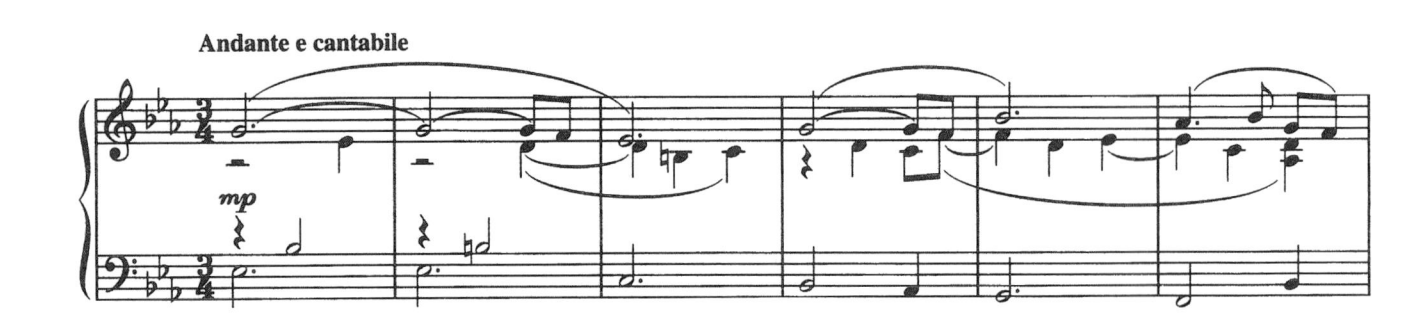

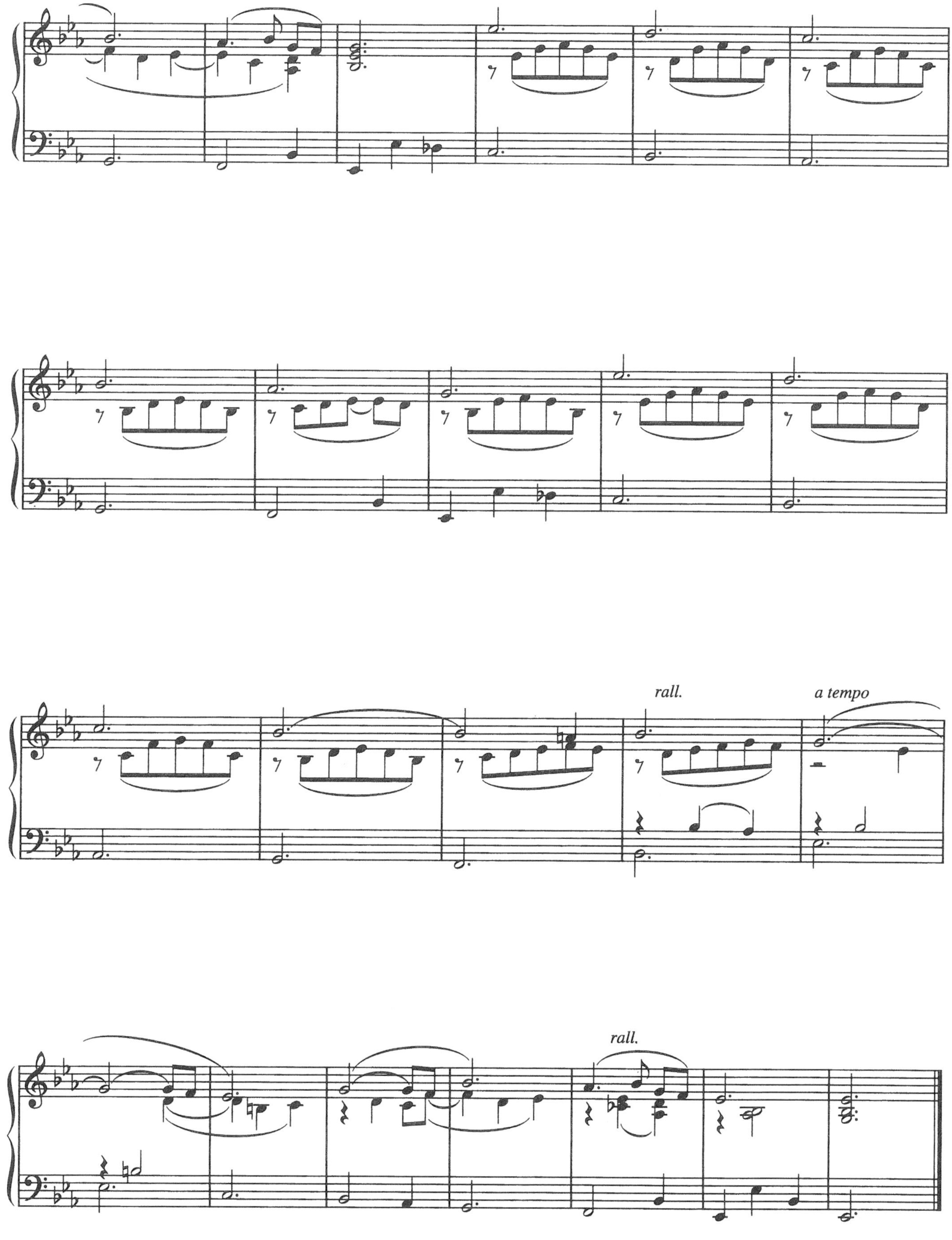
rall.
a tempo
rall.

LAUDATE!

Colin Mawby

© Copyright 1999 Kevin Mayhew Ltd.
It is illegal to photocopy music.

111

PRAYER

Alexandre Guilmant (1837-1911)

113

CANZONA

Gregory Murray (1905-1992)

Moderato

© Copyright 1993 Kevin Mayhew Ltd.
It is illegal photocopy music.

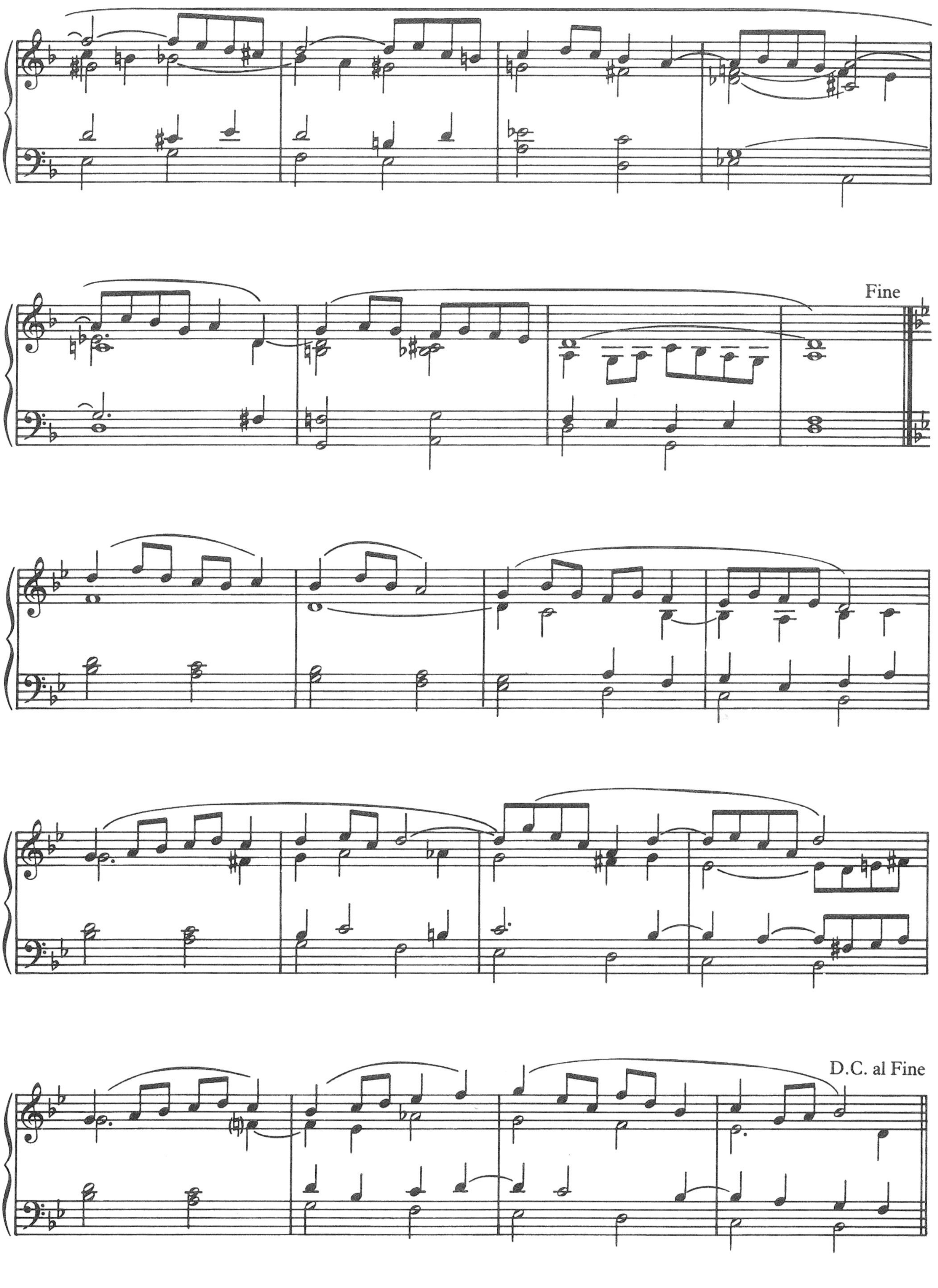
Fine
D.C. al Fine

DILUDIUM
Richard Lloyd

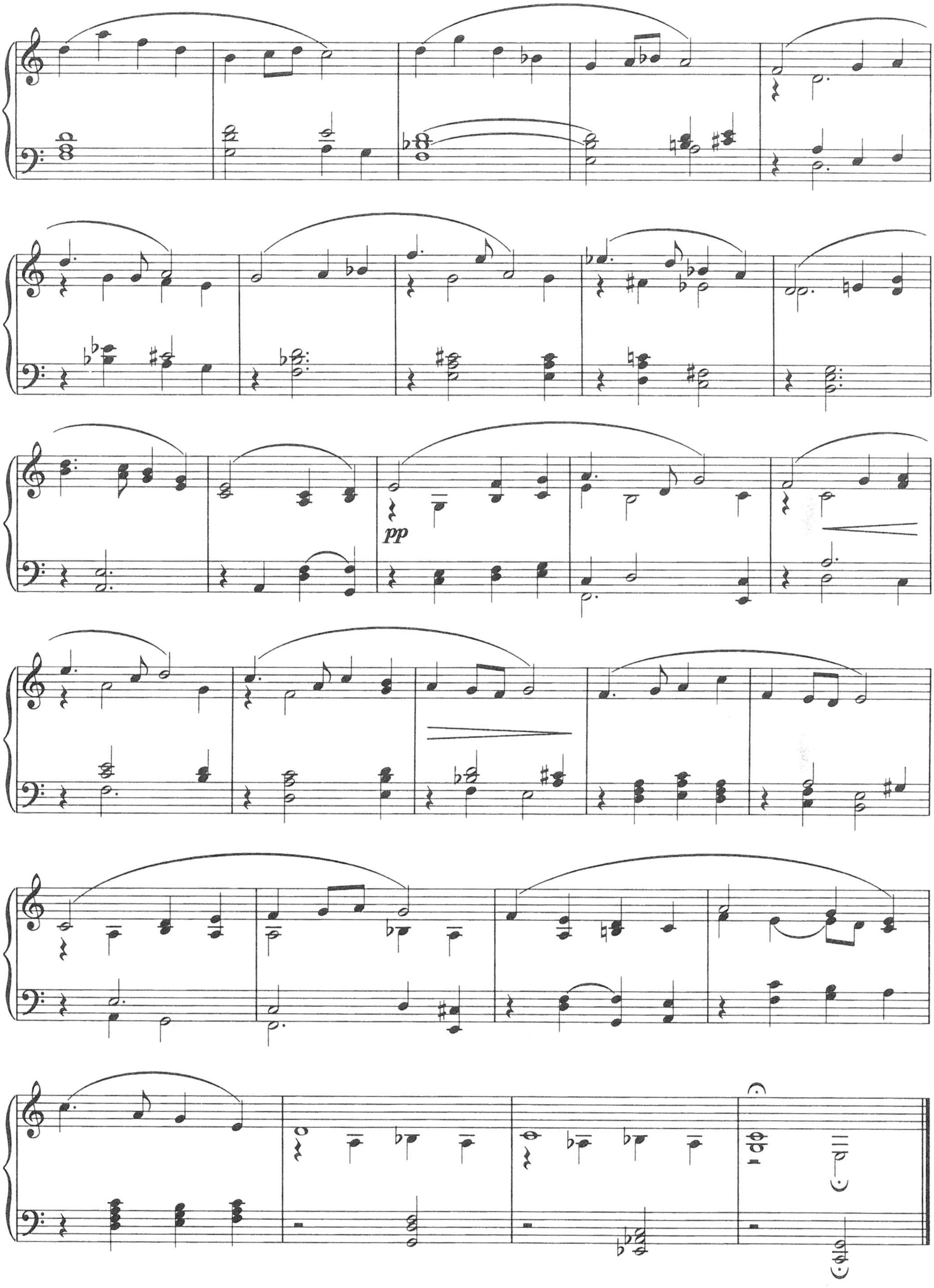
pp

For Dom Paul Eggleston

ANDANTE TRANQUILLO

Andrew Moore

Andante tranquillo

© Copyright 1993 Kevin Mayhew Ltd.
It is illegal photocopy music.

Fine

D.C. al Fine

INTERLUDE

Léon Boëllmann (1862-1897)

121

ELEGY

Michael Higgins

123

A LITTLE JAUNT

Andrew Moore

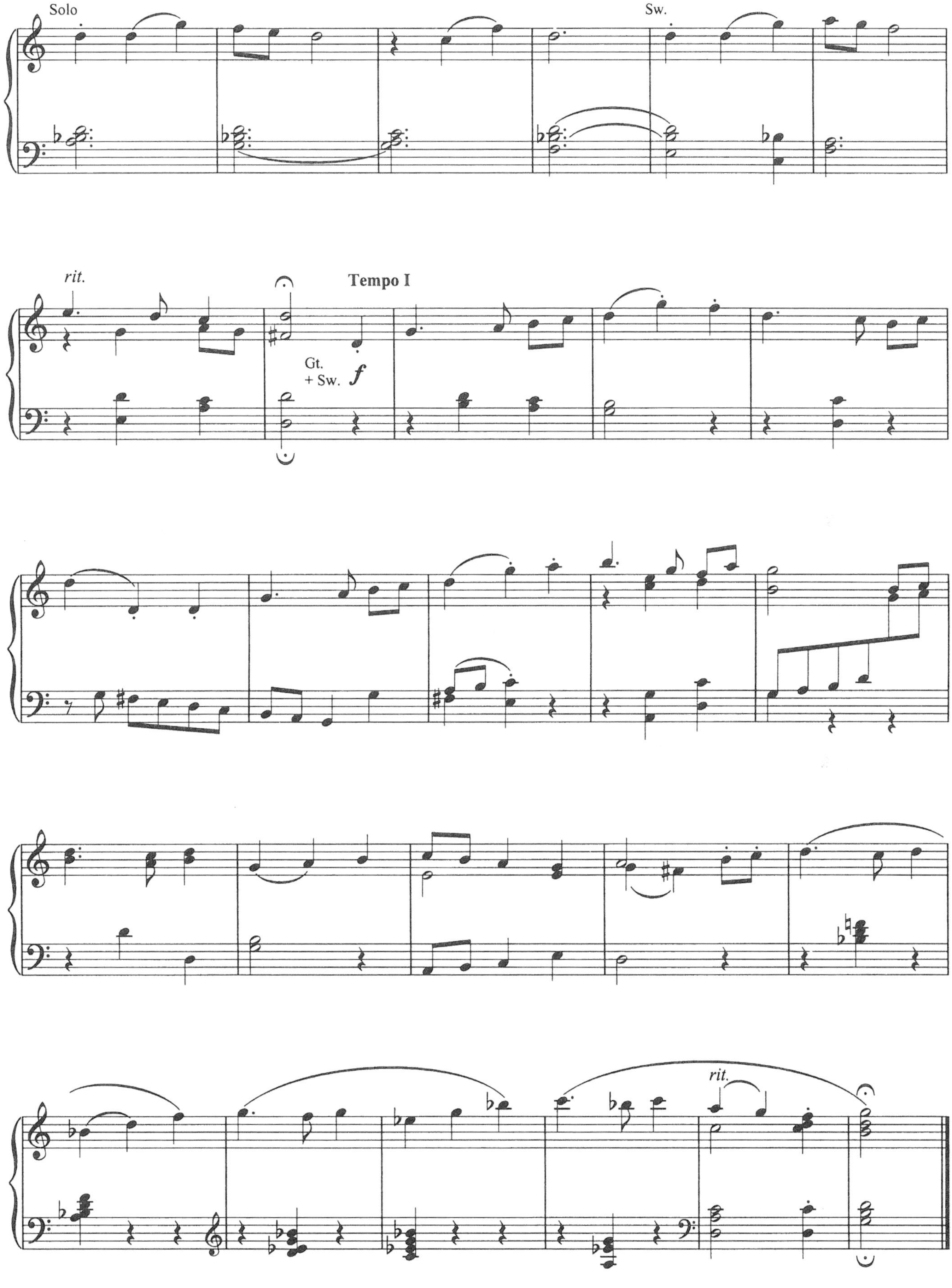
Solo
Sw.
rit.
Tempo I
Gt.
+ Sw.
f
rit.

REFLECTION

Betty Roe

To repeat
Last time
To continue
mp
Fine
mp
pp
p
p
Sw.
mf
mp
mf
rall.
D.C. al Fine

EVENING CALM

Eduard Schütt (1856-1933)